Theory of Education

THE EFFECTIVE TEACHER SERIES

General editor: Elizabeth Perrott

EDUCATION AND CULTURAL DIVERSITY by Edward Hulmes

THE EFFECTIVE TEACHING OF ENGLISH by Robert Protherough, Judith Atkinson and John Fawcett

THEORY OF EDUCATION by Margaret Sutherland

Theory of Education

MARGARET SUTHERLAND

LONGMAN
London and New York

Longman Group UK Limited,
Longman House, Burnt Mill, Harlow,
Essex CM20 2JE, England
and Associated Companies throughout the world.

Published in the United States of America
by Longman Inc., New York

© Longman Group UK Limited 1988

First published 1988

British Library Cataloguing in Publication Data
Sutherland, Margaret
    Theory of education. – (The effective
    teacher).
    I. Title   II. Series
    370'.1   LB1025.2
    ISBN 0-582-29722-2

Library of Congress Cataloging in Publication Data
Sutherland, Margaret B.
    Theory of education.

    (The effective teacher)
    Bibliography: p.
    Includes index.
    1. Teaching. 2. Education – Philosophy. I. Title.
II. Series.
LB1025.2.S948 1988   370'.1   87-22809
ISBN 0-582-29722-2

Set in Linotron 202 10/11pt Times

Produced by Longman Group (FE) Limited
Printed in Hong Kong

CONTENTS

EDITOR'S PREFACE

This new series was inspired by my book on the practice of teaching, (*Effective Teaching: a practical guide to improving your teaching*. Longman 1982) written for teacher training students as well as for in-service teachers wishing to improve their teaching skills. The books in this series have been written with the same readership in mind. However, the busy classroom teacher will also find that the books serve their needs as changes in the nature and pattern of education make the re-training of experienced teachers more essential than in the past.

The rationale behind the series is that professional courses for teachers require the coverage of a wide variety of subjects in a relatively short time. So the aim of the series is the production of 'easy to read', practical guides to provide the necessary subject background, supported by references to encourage and guide further reading together with questions and/or exercises devised to assist application and evaluation.

As specialists in their selected fields, the authors have been chosen for their ability to relate their subjects closely to the needs of teachers and to stimulate discussion of contemporary issues in education.

The series covers subjects ranging from *The Theory of Education* to *The Teaching of Mathematics* and from *The Psychology of Learning* to *Health Education*. It will look at aspects of education as diverse as *Education and Cultural Diversity* and *Assessment in Education, The Teaching of English* and *The History of Education*. Although some titles such as *The Administration of Education* are specific to England and Wales, the majority of titles, such as *Comparative Education, The Teaching of Modern Languages, The Use of Computers in Teaching* and *Pupil Welfare and Counselling* will be international in scope.

In a period when education is a subject of general debate and is operating against a background of major change, there is little doubt that the books, although of primary interest to teachers, will also find a wider readership.

Elizabeth Perrott

AUTHOR'S PREFACE

Ideally, this book should be discussed as it is read. Discussion gives opportunities to make clear anything which at first seems confusing. It allows the reader to suggest other ways in which a theory has obviously been applied or could be applied: it can introduce further examples or criticisms of educational theories or practices. It also helps people to come to their own conclusions. The questions at the end of chapters are intended to encourage such reactions to the text. Thinking about them, individual readers can to some extent interact with the expression of views in the book. Talking about these questions and the different sections or chapters with a group or with individual colleagues or friends still remains helpful.

One of the sometimes annoying things about educational systems is that they keep changing. By the time this book reaches the reader, government decisions may have altered some of the provisions for education in different parts of the world. This does not greatly matter, since it does not affect the underlying principles. Indeed it may be useful to look at such changes and see which educational theory may support or oppose them.

The number of books for further reading has deliberately been kept to a minimum. There are many other books on the topics referred to, but those recommended do seem worth reading and will indicate other books and journals concerning education or the social sciences associated with them.

The need to present many theories in a limited number of words has meant that sometimes the book sounds more dogmatic than it is meant to be. The reader's own critical judgement will decide what is generally established and what stems from the author's own personal preferences. Again, this is where discussion has merits – I wish I could participate in it.

Margaret Sutherland

CHAPTER 1

Theories of education

If teaching is to be a self-respecting and respected profession, every teacher should have a theory of education. Teachers should know clearly what they are trying to achieve, why they teach certain things to pupils, why they use certain methods of teaching. It is not always as easy as one would expect to be clear on these matters. We are confronted by many ideas about education, by people who have conflicting proposals as to what should be done. Somehow we have to evaluate these and decide on our own theory.

Theories do make a difference. The popular cliché that something is 'all very well in theory, no good in practice' is nonsense: theory of education comes from thinking about real events. If some ideas about education do not have the expected results when they are put into practice they must be changed or rejected – provided that they really have been given a fair trial and have not been distorted when they were applied because their user misunderstood them. For example, it may be claimed that the theory of the project method does not work since projects do not improve children's ability to find things out for themselves and remember what they have found: but then we discover that children said to be taught by the project method were not given the chance to choose the topic to be studied – i.e. to form their own project: they were merely told to go and look up information on a topic chosen by the teacher. The theory holds that children working on a topic which interests them will show initiative and determination in finding out and learning about it: work directed by the teacher without reference to the children's interests does not use or test the theory here. We have to be sure exactly which theory has been used in education: and indeed whether a theory has been used.

EFFECTS OF THEORIES

We can see the results of different theories of education in classrooms, schools and social life at present and in the past. If the theory is that children have limited ability to think things out for themselves and are naturally badly behaved, then educators give firm guidance and supervision and try to ensure that children learn what adults think good for them – 'children should be seen and not heard', children must use their childhood preparing to become respectable adults and good workers, even if they find the process uncomfortable. If the theory is that education must make children good members of a special kind of society, the subjects and methods of education are developed accordingly. Quite recently, Nazi education offered a striking example: children were to learn to believe in the goodness of the Nazi state and the superiority of the Aryan race: the curriculum presented history, geography and science modified to support these views, physical education was emphasized (to produce healthy citizens and soldiers), youth organisations were created to encourage feelings of group membership, loyalty to the state, readiness to denounce and destroy its enemies. Variants of such a theory and educational methods can be noted in various countries of the world today. But other theories emphasize that education in childhood should be a time of happiness when children have freedom to develop their inborn abilities and follow their own interests: so 'play-way' methods are used, self-expression is fostered and pupils can choose what to study and what to do. An attempt is being made by the Council of Europe to draw up a charter of children's rights: such rights can be far-reaching, e.g. in Sweden children have the legal right to object to some forms of parental discipline and to ask to be put into the care of other 'parents'. Such recognitions of children's rights obviously rest on an important theory of education. Religious beliefs also determine education: various groups have held that the essential in education is to ensure that children learn about their religion, behave according to its teaching and remain devoted followers of their religion: other studies are not important in comparison with these and methods are likely to develop obedience and acceptance rather than independence of thinking. We can see such education in some Christian sects and in other world religions both in the past and the present.

QUESTIONS RELATED TO THEORIES

Given such varieties of beliefs about education, the teacher has to decide which, if any, of such views to accept. Is education to prepare the child for adult life; to prepare citizens of a clearly defined political state; to make children happy and allow them to decide their own learning; to ensure their moral and religious goodness? But teachers are not the only educators. What happens if children's parents have views different from those of the teacher? Do parents have an absolute right to decide their children's education? Why – or why not? Should children be allowed to opt out of their parents' care and opinions and beliefs? Should children's rights be internationally defined and be the same and respected in all countries? All these are questions of theory of education.

But can a theory of education be regarded as having the same authority as scientific theories? Usually what people have in mind here is that a scientific theory is one based on controlled experiments and observations. They rather expect laboratories where people in white coats take accurate measurements of the results of carefully defined operations. Certainly the more important aspects of education cannot be treated in this way (though some aspects of learning can be 'scientifically' assessed). There are so many variables which come into educational activities – a child's state of health, the influence of the home background, the child's reaction to a particular teacher, the length of time during which learning will be effective, attitudes to learning, the child's expectations, the quality of materials used – these cannot all be effectively controlled and assessed. So theories of education cannot be based on 'scientific' experiments of the kind used in some physical sciences.

Even so, some progress has been made in studying education in the systematic way just indicated. Children and young people can be observed methodically in a number of situations where they are treated differently by those around them: they can be observed in different countries which have their own distinctive ways of providing education and the apparent results of these different systems can be compared. This methodical and, so far as possible, unbiased observation and assessment may give guidance as to whether the theories of education used in different circumstances are having the effects expected and hoped for. If careful observation and thought suggest that the real situation does not correspond to what was expected, then the theory can be modified or its application changed. This is, in fact, what happens also in the physical sciences and other sciences. All scientific theories are subject to modification or rejection as new observations and new ideas are applied to them. The new theories are then checked and modified in their turn. Even the theory of gravity is at present being critically reconsidered.

TWO IMPORTANT CHARACTERISTICS OF THEORIES OF EDUCATION

There are two respects in which theories of education must indeed differ from 'scientific' theories. One is that there are limits to the kinds of experiments we can carry out with human beings.

The story is told that centuries ago a Scottish king tried to discover whether human beings have an innate knowledge of language, that language being the language of the Garden of Eden: if left to develop without interference they might use that language. So this king is said to have put a new-born baby to be cared for by a deaf-mute woman on an otherwise uninhabited island. Unfortunately, perhaps, the results of this experiment do not seem to have been written up: but we can imagine the outcry if such an experiment were attempted today. Parents who shut children away from normal human contact are regarded with horror and the children are usually removed from their care. Even less drastic experiments are stopped by society: and the present disputes about work producing 'test tube babies' show the abhorrence felt at the idea of experimenting on human beings. Experiments on human beings are irreversible: the material used cannot be simply discarded once the experiment is over (though 'medical' researchers in Nazi concentration camps were apparently ready to do just this). So there are limits to what can be 'tried out' as methods of education, even if it is sometimes hard to define these limits.

Secondly, in theory of education we make value judgements. We know what we want the results to be, whereas the research worker in the physical sciences is concerned simply to know what the results are if certain interventions are made. Therefore our theory is not simply a statement about what is: theory of education is a statement of what should happen and which actions are most likely to bring about this effect (actions being modified when they demonstrably do not bring about the intended effect). So an essential difference between educational and 'scientific' theory remains. While a theory of education may be modified with respect to methods of achieving the intended results it is improbable that the initial value judgement about aims will change. (Sometimes observation and experience of the effects of education in given circumstances can cause the educator to revise the basic value judgements: but this happens only rarely – perhaps it should happen more frequently.)

PRACTICAL CONSIDERATIONS FOR TEACHERS

Do teachers have time to think about theory? Is it worth while for them to do so? If we consider the everyday circumstances of the teacher's work, it looks as though other people decide largely what the good teacher is expected to do. School reports and prospectuses show the importance attached to pupils' examination performance: so teachers have to think about how to get good exam results. Heads of schools and heads of departments indicate what is to be taught and, often, how it is to be taught. Parents expect pupils to be prepared to get a good job (even in the present state of the economy parents still expect their children to find employment): so teachers have to attend to this objective, trying to ensure that the child is well advised which courses to follow and how to set about getting a job. Some schools emphasise achievement in sports – though some teachers may decide this is not their concern. Inspectors and Advisers make comments on and recommendations about the teacher's work – and more systematic appraisal of individual teacher performance seems likely to be extended. Every now and then new subjects are introduced while other subjects are edged out – e.g. the newly arrived computer studies and the vanishing study of Latin. New examinations with new syllabuses are brought into existence: teachers have to cope, somehow, with these. Local authorities make rulings and determine teachers' conditions of work, for instance, with regard to supervision of school meals, or covering for colleagues who are absent. School governors are given various powers to decide what is done in the school and how its work is to proceed: parental involvement is advocated so that parents' views also may influence the daily activities of the school. In this maelstrom of demands and directives, has the teacher any opportunity to think about and act on an individual theory?

There is too the question of time span. Theory of education is concerned with long-term effects: the desired outcome of good education takes a long time to be produced. It also depends on the efforts of more than one person. The teacher is in contact with children or young people during only limited periods of time and during a small number of years. So the teacher is likely to focus on only some aspects of education, those that make immediate demands and are within the control of the individual teacher. Much of the teacher's planning has to be short-term. What activity is to be undertaken this week – or this period? Indeed, what action is to be taken during the next quarter-of-an-hour to prevent the last period on a wet Friday afternoon from developing into a riot situation? When the teacher assesses the effects of teaching, that too is likely to be on a short-term basis – what has been learned this week, this term or this year? It seems to be not so much a matter of whether the class is now generally competent and enthusiastic but whether it has acquired some basic information or skill. What has happened to last year's learners, now that the teacher no longer is responsible for them, may seem a pointless question, certainly not one with a high priority among demands on the teacher's attention. One of the most frustrating but little mentioned characteristics of the teacher's work is indeed to see a class which has been well taught and has responded with enthusiasm, being 'put off' by having an indifferent teacher during the following year so that its perform-ance degenerates and pupils move towards dropping some subjects (if at the options stage) and some even become anti-school. The standards or behaviour developed by the hard work of the individual teacher are undermined and lost by the weak-ness or indifference of less keen colleagues. It depends, of course, on how much cooperation and common interest there is in a school staff – and that depends on the staff's theory or theories of education. But one must recognise the pressures towards keeping the individual teacher's attention and efforts within narrow limits.

THE IMPORTANCE OF TEACHERS' THEORIES

Yet even in deterrent circumstances teachers do remain concerned about the long-term effects of their work. No one likes to be regarded simply as a child-minder whose function it is to keep children or young people quiet and out of the way until they are old enough to be let loose as members of the adult community. Teachers do pride themselves on being rather more than jailers: and they do not see themselves as mere mechanics following someone else's specifications. They claim that the activities of the classroom and school are not time-filling devices: they are activities of value for the pupils, activities which will continue to be of value after the pupils have left school. Other-wise what claim would teachers have to the respect of society? How would they justify – to bring the argument to a lower plane – the payment of good salaries if what they teach is not of real value to the learners? Teachers have to think about the long-term effects of their work even if, from day to day, most of their attention must be given to short-term decisions. And the work itself must stimulate them to consider long-term effects as they notice pupils' reactions to it, hear pupils' questions and become aware of the other influences which are affecting their pupils' behaviour and attitudes. Being a teacher must make the indi-vidual think about the nature of the human beings who are being taught and what values that experience has and should have for them. Individual teachers inevitably do have a theory of education even if it is seldom explicit and not necessarily consistent.

There are other more dramatic occasions when teachers' views on the purposes of education become clear and are of major importance. When Nazi politicians tried to introduce into the curriculum of schools information which teachers knew to be false, when they proposed to distort historical and biological knowledge, many teachers resisted either by refusing to teach such material or by leaving the profession: they would not have false aims substituted for those they held valuable. Japanese teachers who disapproved of the official teaching about the primacy of the state in the pre-war years showed their unwillingness to accept the role of propagators of such doctrines by insisting in years following the Second World War that moral education should not be given in schools but at home – thus trying to avoid the use of the schools for propaganda purposes. Within schools one can see how, on occasion, teachers who feel strongly that the school policy is wrong insist on an enquiry and/or a change of policy – one could say that the Tyndale case in England, when complaints were made by teachers that the *laissez faire* attitudes of some colleagues were preventing children from deriving benefit from school, was an instance of teachers' awareness of the consequences of erroneous theories and their determination that children should not suffer because of a mistaken choice of theory.

The question is, who should judge of the rightness of a theory of education or of proposals for change in education? As we have noted, innovations and changes are incessantly being introduced into the school system, sometimes on a major scale, sometimes with lesser effects. The introduction of comprehensive schools in 1965 was one of the greatest changes: the new English GCSE examination could also rank as a far-reaching change. Yet the views of the teaching profession have scarcely been determining factors in these operations. In other instances we have complaints by parents about sex education or political studies in schools or politicians disapprove of peace studies. Again, there may be conflicting decisions by boards of governors and committees of the local authority as when in a recent case school governors and many teachers thought that pupils who had written obscene graffiti about teachers should be expelled while the local authority wanted the pupils reinstated. In such cases, when any changes are proposed for education it is the teachers who should be looked to for a professional judgement as to the merits of the proposal. But such professional judgement can be respected only if teachers have thought systematically about the purposes of education, have considered and evaluated the principles which underlie the competing proposals and have checked the resulting ideas against their own experience of teaching. It is unlikely that such judgements will be accepted without argument by all the others concerned. But teachers professionally trained in such matters are better able to distinguish whether proposals are based on reasonable theories or are simply the expression of unthinking prejudices or an attempt to climb on a political bandwagon. It may be that not all teachers will accept the same educational aims and methods: but after systematic, professional study they will have much in common and will be better able to understand and reason with those holding other views. Teachers indeed, as a professional group, should not be simply passive acceptors of proposals made by others or assessors of others' views but should be ready to propose also those changes which they can see as helpful to the development of all education. At the same time, if teachers are to be assessed either by others within the profession or by outsiders, it is essential that they should be able to say what are the professional principles on which they are working and assessment of their work should be related to these principles.

DECIDING ON A THEORY OF EDUCATION

How are teachers to arrive at this professional competence and establish their claim to be consulted and to have their judgement respected? They can do much by simply thinking about their own everyday experience and discussing it – seriously – with colleagues: but their own experience can be made more comprehensible and useful if they also compare it with what other people have thought and discovered about education. That is why it is important to consider some of the major existing theories of education, what various people have written about the process of educating and what action they have taken or recommended. This does not mean that there is any particular merit in simply knowing what other people's theories of education are. Studying them is useful when it makes clearer to us how far we agree and how far we do not agree with the views that have been put forward by others. In some cases, opinions that have been expressed in the past may not seem relevant to present conditions: then we have to decide whether the general principle was at fault or whether it was simply a matter of methods which must change to adapt to modern conditions. In general, it is probable that we find, in thinking about what other people have written about education, considerable agreement in their judgements of what the ideal outcome of education would be. In other cases, we find that we do reject some concepts of the ideal outcome: but even studying these theories has value because, in deciding to reject such views, we become clearer as to what our own views are and what arguments can be used to justify our own views. So the following chapters will include the views of a variety of people who have written about the purposes of education and the methods by which these purposes can be worked out in practice, as well as examples of education in practice in different circumstances.

These views are not presented for automatic acceptance or for memorising. They are offered as encouragement to individuals to decide how acceptable other people's theories of education are and how far they coincide with the individual's own thinking.

Questions

1. What characteristics do people expect in a scientific theory?

2. Why is it difficult for a theory of education to be 'scientific' in the usually accepted sense of the word?

3. What pressures make it difficult for teachers to think about the long-term effects of education?

4. What theories of education seem to influence the school system at present?

5. Why is it important for the teacher to have a theory of education?

CHAPTER 2

The child-centred approach

Are children naturally good? Will they learn if they are not compelled to learn? What will they learn if they are given a free choice? Can we rely on their inborn interests and abilities?

These are questions which have been answered in one way by traditional educators and in another way by child-centred educators. Usually it is taken for granted that children should learn what adults think it is good for them to learn. The methods used and the timetable also depend on the opinions and judgement of adults. Child-centred educators argue that by this approach we don't give children a chance to develop as well as they could: we crush or distort their real abilities and interests. We make education a time of unhappiness instead of the joyful and rewarding time it ought to be. So what attitudes and actions are proposed in child-centred education?

THE BEGINNINGS OF CHILD-CENTRED EDUCATION

Child-centred education is probably easier to understand if we look at the ideas presented by Jean-Jacques Rousseau who is generally credited with having introduced this theory of education. In his book *Emile*, published in 1762,[1] he asserted that we should not begin by concentrating on the vast amount of information that we want children to acquire, we should rather begin by considering what the child is capable of learning and what the child is interested in learning. Instead of beginning from the outside – from subjects and skills which adults think important – we should begin from what is already in the child, the capacity to develop. We then find that some activities and studies suit the child at different stages. We should provide for these: education will then ensure the development of a good human being, one who has enjoyed learning, is keen to continue to learn and is a responsible member of society.

STAGES OF DEVELOPMENT

From his own observations, Rousseau claimed to distinguish four main stages of development which did not necessarily have sharply defined age limits but were characterised by different abilities and interests. These were the stage of infancy, from birth to two years approximately; the stage of childhood, from 2 to 12; the stage of pre-adolescence, from twelve to fifteen; and the stage of adolescence from 15 into early adulthood. (In our own time, another Swiss, Jean Piaget, has made popular a similar view of stages of development and their characteristics.) The most radical of Rousseau's proposals were for education during childhood. This should *not* be a time for learning from books or studying words: it is a time for learning by physical activity and real experience. During these years the child should develop physical skills and sense discrimination, since these are natural growth areas. The child should be much out of doors, playing, enjoying physical activity. Singing may be learned and possibly a little reading and writing: but reading and writing should be only for such things as personal correspondence: the child should not read books. This is because, according to Rousseau, books can be read by children without any real understanding of their contents. Children, in his view, have the ability to 'parrot' what they read or hear and so adults think that children are learning when the children are simply repeating empty sounds: the children have no concepts of the true meanings of the words or have distorted and imperfect concepts. Thus the child can be given an unreal, misleading view of the world. 'I hate books!' wrote Rousseau (presumably only in this context since he did produce quite a few books himself). The child's thinking at this stage is rather to be stimulated by physical activity and by observation of the immediate environment.

At the next stage, pre-adolescence, Rousseau proposed to continue the emphasis on learning actively, by first-hand experience. The child is now at a stage when interest in the physical environment is lively: so study of scientific and geographical principles can begin, through carefully arranged situations in which the child meets with a problem which has to be solved – e.g. to find the right way home through a wood the child has to notice the growth of moss on trees to know which is north, south, and so on. One book is now allowed: *Robinson Crusoe*, which shows what skills and knowledge are necessary if the human being is to survive in the natural world. Thinking about Crusoe's experience, the learner can judge the value of various skills and pieces of knowledge: the criterion is their usefulness in ensuring the individual's survival. The learner also should acquire at this stage a practical craft skill, not only for immediate use but, as the learner will also discover, as a means of making a useful contribution to society, serving the well-being of others and being accepted by them.

Despite this strictly limited access to the knowledge available in books during the early stages of education, Rousseau's pupil would, in later adolescence, rapidly catch up with more conventional subjects of study, reading works of history, philosophy, literature, receiving sex education and acquiring an understanding of religion – to the horror of orthodox people of the time, Rousseau firmly excluded religion from education until this stage, arguing, as later writers have done, that the child's mind is not able to understand religious teaching about God and morality in the earlier stages of development. The acceptance of considerable study of books in adolescence was based on the view that by now the individual is interested in relationships with others, is capable of understanding such relationships and can therefore benefit by reading books which give insight into the behaviour of other human beings. The study of political and economic circumstances in other countries is also appropriate now since the adolescent has to decide which is the best society to live in.

It will be evident that the new view of education did not apply only to cognitive learning. Rousseau made equally radical proposals concerning character development. He rejected traditional views that human beings are naturally wicked and so must have their behaviour corrected from birth onwards: natural impulses, in his view, are good. He rejected verbal teaching about what is right and wrong and the use of punishment by adults to make the child behave well. Again he argued that the child cannot really understand many of the moral rules propounded by adults. If the child thinks something is wrong because adults disapprove of it, the child's reaction is to conceal the behaviour from adults and, if challenged, to deny it (even if adults have said that it is wrong to tell lies).

DISCIPLINE OF NATURAL CONSEQUENCES

Nevertheless, Rousseau did accept the value of one kind of discipline for children, the discipline of natural consequences. The failure of many attempts to improve children's behaviour may, he thought, be due to the artificial nature of punishments: children come to believe that punishment is arbitrary, a matter of adults' whims: consequently, the child reasons, if adult knowledge of the behaviour can be prevented, there is no good reason to avoid the behaviour itself. (Similar reasoning is still evident in many delinquents' points of view in our own time.) What Rousseau proposed was that the child should learn about cause and effect in any course of action: the child should discover that certain actions have – naturally and inevitably – unpleasant consequences: so the child will refrain from these actions in future. Rousseau offered a perhaps rather feeble example of making the child suffer the consequences of breaking a window: staying in a room where the wind and rain can come in because the window panes don't offer protection should make it clear to the child that breaking windows is something to be avoided. This understanding is much more likely to affect the child's future behaviour than some irrelevant punishment accompanied by the instant repair of the window.

Of course Rousseau and other child-centred educators would not take this policy to absurd lengths. Some actions have irreversible consequences: the child who goes swimming in a dangerous river may not live to profit by the lesson learned: similarly, the child who experiments today with probing live electric sockets may receive an excessively effective final lesson. But the child-centred educator thinks it important to ensure that the child realises the consequences of actions. The child thus learns that certain actions are bad because they produce bad consequences. Such learning is much more effective than discipline imposed from outside. If adult sanctions are seen as the main deterrent, then – if the forbidden action is otherwise attractive – the obvious thing to do is to ensure that adults don't know what is going on. But if the learner knows that the action itself, however superficially attractive, is bound to have punitive consequences, then the action will be avoided.

Even so, Rousseau did recognise another way in which, at a later stage of development, behaviour may be controlled. It is by a kind of innate conscience. Given his belief in the natural goodness of the human being, Rousseau argued that if the human being is well educated and protected from corrupting influences during the formative years the human being can be guided by an inner feeling – consult the heart – and this inner feeling will spontaneously judge what is right and what is wrong. This, rather than a conventional religious doctrine, is the best guarantee of moral behaviour on the part of the correctly educated human being.

LATER DEVELOPMENTS OF CHILD-CENTRED EDUCATION

Other child-centred authorities have adapted, modified or extended the principles originally put forward by Rousseau. Froebel, whose ideas led to the establishment of kindergartens, emphasised the importance of children's play. Adults had earlier viewed this activity with tolerance but as something unimportant. Froebel saw it as the way in which the child naturally learns to understand the world. He suggested that by providing suitable toys and games, educators can encourage this natural way of understanding physical objects and their properties. Play also allows the expression of the child's own ideas.

Froebel and other child-centred educators used the metaphor of the gardener and plant to illustrate this theory of education. 'Kindergarten', the word that Froebel's work introduced into the English language, indeed means 'garden of children'. The metaphor suggests that educators, like gardeners, must have faith in their charges' capacity to grow into good specimens of their kind. The gardener provides a suitable environment and protects against damage but growth and blossoming come from within the plant. This faith in the goodness of natural development is characteristic of the child-centred approach. It is believed that if people are allowed to develop freely, they will develop well. This attitude to the child is well crystallised in Wordsworth's phrase 'trailing clouds of glory do we come' (though the rest of Wordsworth's philosophy might not be accepted by all child-centred educators). So the role of the educator is like that of the gardener, to provide a suitable environment and nourishment for the natural development of the individual.

To this a further important principle is linked: education should be a happy experience for the child. Rousseau denounced the education of his day which made children miserable on the assumption that they were thus being prepared for a happy, or at least a successful, adult life. (He would not accept the phrase popular with some parents urging children to do homework or other unwelcome tasks, 'You'll be glad one day that I made you do it'.) It is wrong and unnecessary, he argued, to sacrifice the child's present happiness for the sake of a hypothetical future – an argument all the more telling at his time when so many children died before reaching adult life. Other like-minded educators have emphasised this enjoyment of the present in education. It is not that the educator sets out simply to produce happiness: but if the educator provides for activities that suit the child's development and interests, education must be a time of happiness. Education which forces on the child the learning of things which are irrelevant (from the child's point of view) or beyond the child's understanding, will inevitably be an unhappy experience.

WHAT IS 'NATURAL'?

In all this we must wonder what is meant by natural development. A great deal depends on the environment in which the individual, or the plant, grows. Even in the situation of the gardener and plant we know that conditions in the environment may inhibit or speed up some plants' flowering. Some plants may never bloom in certain environments: how is the observer there to know what their 'nature' is? Some plants may badly affect others by claiming available water, shade, light: in so doing they are following their natural tendencies: but what might the natural development of their neighbours otherwise have been? If we abandon the metaphor (and metaphors are a bad way of arguing in education and elsewhere) and look at children's 'natural' environments in the modern world we can see how widely they differ – urban, rural, inner city, sparsely populated areas, life in a small group of people, at home, in a community or in a large institution. These factors must affect the way in which the child will develop. The selection of activities available in the child's immediate surroundings will inevitably determine which interests the child will express or want to cultivate. Interests natural to a child brought up in a large city of the Western world may be quite different from those 'natural' to a child brought up in an Eskimo community or a child growing up in a shanty town in South America. So does the natural development of the child really depend on what the educator offers in the way of environment and resources? Not so, the child-centred educator would argue: in any environments there will be common reactions and enthusiasms among children: the stages of development will be the same. The child-centred educator focuses on such common characteristics even if it is recognised that some environments give little scope for their expression. Enjoyment of physical activities in the early years, curiosity, the wish to explore the environment, creative ability, enthusiasm for learning, expression of the individual's own personality – these, it is argued, are natural in all human beings and are too often inhibited by traditional, intellectual, bookish education.

But another problem in interpreting what is 'natural' arises when we think about social behaviour. The discipline of natural consequences may well be used when the child is dealing with objects in the material environment. It is harder to use effectively when it is a matter of dealing with other people. Rousseau held that adult anger and displeasure are not effective deterrent consequences for the child and that they should not be used as the natural consequences of certain actions. But later writers, for example, Herbert Spencer,[2] have argued that it is reasonable for the adult to show by coldness or withdrawal of affection that certain behaviour is unacceptable. Other child-centred educators have accepted that disapproval expressed by the group, preferably by the peer group, is a 'natural' and highly effective consequence. (Rousseau's views were perhaps distorted by the fact that he thought of his ideal pupil being mainly in the company of a tutor or of parents: he therefore omitted to consider the social education which children receive from mixing with other children.)

SOCIAL DISCIPLINE

We do indeed find the reactions of a group deliberately used by some child-centred educators to serve as an effective sanction against anti-social behaviour. For example, early this century, Homer Lane's farm community,[3] The Little Commonwealth, attempted to reform young delinquents partly through meetings of the 'citizens' at which discussions about individual behaviour, as well as general matters affecting the community, took place. The citizens themselves decided which behaviours were acceptable and made their own rules. For example, rushing through houses at night, slamming doors, was ruled unacceptable since it interfered with others' sleep. (Yet a more impersonal form of discipline by 'natural' consequences was used in the community: the Little Commonwealth had a token currency of its own so that those who worked were paid and could use the currency to buy additional food or other desirable commodities. Hence the connection between work and reward was clear. But some personal group influences entered here also since the citizens lived in a number of quite small houses and if one person in the house avoided work, the others could complain that their standard of living was lowered – no jam for tea, for example!)

Similarly, A S Neill's school, Summerhill,[4] developed the system of general meetings in which anyone can bring a complaint against the behaviour of any other in the school community (teachers included): penalties are imposed by the community.

In these ways, individuals brought up in child-centred environments discover that some forms of behaviour have social consequences, the displeasure of others. It appears an effective way of learning. It can, on occasion, also occur in school classes. Yet while child-centred educators apparently accept that such group reactions are natural consequences and experiencing them is part of natural development, the emotional reaction of an adult to bad behaviour on the part of children is less clearly acceptable and is, on the whole, deprecated.

Anti-social behaviour can thus be reformed by natural learning experiences. But if human nature is, as the child-centred educators assert, naturally good, how does anti-social behaviour, delinquency, crime arise? For the child-centred educator such behaviour shows that naturally good impulses have not been allowed to find expression; they have been discouraged, neglected, frustrated so that they express themselves in undesirable ways. Froebel[5] was one of the earliest to point out how, for instance, the young child wants to join in parents' work, to help in it – a naturally good impulse: but because the child is unskilful or gets in the way, adults reject the offered help: and later, when the child's help would be useful, they complain that the child is selfish, unwilling to cooperate. Froebel also pointed out that the child's actions are often misjudged: the child does not always foresee the consequences of actions and may be as horrified as adults at the results of well-intentioned behaviour: but the child is believed to have intended these results and so acquires a bad reputation, a poor self-concept, and then lives up, or down, to that reputation.

Homer Lane expressed this view[6] particularly strongly when he rejoiced in some delinquents' aggressive attitude to authority. This showed, he believed, the unconquered human spirit seeking a freedom which had earlier been unreasonably denied to it.

Whatever the degree of confidence one may place in such interpretations, it is important to note that this belief in natural goodness has led many child-centred educators to work hard, often in highly unattractive conditions, to re-educate delinquent or maladjusted young people, believing that an appropriate education will allow past frustrations and misdirections to work themselves out, so that the individual finds equilibrium and there-after behaves in accordance with basically good human nature

Yet the freedom of such a group to be self-regulating is not always appreciated by the group. David Wills reported[7] an inter-esting example of such reactions in his book, *The Barns Experiment*. Boys in this residential school had been sent there because, as wartime evacuees, they had proved to be unaccept-able in ordinary families. The school developed the system of having a committee of the boys which determined rules and imposed sanctions on offenders. But at one stage the committee decided that it was all too much work and they voted – duly following accepted committee procedure – to abolish the committee and the system. Wills accepted this but replaced this committee self-governing arrangement by a dictatorship of his own, though he told the boys that his dictatorship, unlike others, could be abolished when they felt ready to take back the responsibility for governing themselves. In due course, they did so. Yet this instance highlights a point not often enough recog-nised – that thinking about other people's behaviour as well as one's own, and trying to maintain the rules that a group has agreed on, can be a wearisome process. Groups, like indi-viduals, may sometimes find it more restful to be told what to do. Freedom involves making choices and ensuring that they are adhered to. The reaction of Wills' committee resembles the un-happy query of a child in a 'free activity' school: 'Do I *have* to choose what to do again today?' The underlying question is whether the human being always wants freedom to choose or whether sometimes impulses arising spontaneously – or failing to arise – are happily replaced by guidance from outside: it may of course be a matter of earlier experience of freedom, or denial of freedom to choose, which affects subsequent behaviour. We are again confronted by the question of what is 'natural' to human beings.

CHILD-CENTRED METHODS AND MATERIALS IN TEACHING

The main principles of child-centred education so far noted are those of giving the child freedom to develop naturally and avoiding limiting the child's activity by adult prejudices, adult rules and adult choices of subjects to be learned. This theory of education has emphasised not only a new kind of discipline and a new definition of what is to be learned but it has also changed the methods and materials used in education.

Learning by experience

Rousseau advocated learning by experience so that the child's knowledge is not at the verbal level but is founded on real observations and perceptions. This gives the child a better base for later thinking since the concepts will be accurate and thus capable of further development. Observation of objects and events in their natural environment has become a characteristic of child-centred education, going back to the time of Pestalozzi who described[8] how the ideal mother, Gertrude, living in a small village, taught her children and others by using the everyday furnishings of the home, for example, teaching them to count by counting window-panes. This emphasis on observing and using real objects led to the formal 'object lessons' which became popular in nineteenth- and early twentieth-century education when some object was presented to a class so that its characteristics could be carefully observed and described. A stuffed bird, for instance, might be brought into the classroom and the pupils led to 'observe' such things as the shape of its feet and beak, and so to deduce the conditions in which it had lived and found food: or its distinctive or protective colouring might be admired. Perhaps children did learn a lot from such lessons: this was, to some extent, progress from mere words in books or even from the use of pictures in books, which had been an earlier attempt to make learning relate to real objects. But this teaching device was still far removed from first-hand experience which would observe living birds in their natural habitat. We take this principle of learning nearer to the ideal in today's 'nature tables' in primary classrooms, in having pet animals in schools, in nature walks, visits to nature reserves and other school journeys: or in visits to buildings or assemblies of special interest. (The status of television viewing as a kind of 'real' experience is uncertain. Certainly it gives a number of real perceptions of appearance, colour, sound, movement, environments and so seems to provide material for accurate concept formation. Yet it does not have the same qualities as events in the individual's own life.)

Discovery methods

In a rather different way the introduction of 'discovery methods' in science teaching in schools is part of the child-centred approach. The individual is given the opportunity to experiment with materials, to discover what happens in response to chosen manipulations. Thus scientific principles become not something learned from a textbook or by watching other people's experiments but something the individual has discovered by initiating activities, observing and interpreting their results. Such learning is likely to be more clearly remembered than 'passive' learning or learning by simply following someone else's directions. It may lead to further discovery and experiment for the individual is said to discover in this way not only the properties of the materials worked with but the possibility of thinking things out, arriving at independent results and conclusions. The development of creative ideas or other creative behaviour is expected to be helped by such foundations of experience, observation, personal involvement.

Books

Child-centred ideas have also changed books and teaching materials. Great efforts – which we now tend to take for granted – have been made to suit what are believed to be the learner's abilities and interests at a given stage. Few, if any, child-centred educators follow Rousseau in banishing books from the young child's learning experience but it has been recognised that we must check whether written material really is comprehensible: so the vocabulary, sentence structures, illustrations of books intended for children are analysed. Materials presented in them – and exam questions used to test learning from them – are scrutinised to discover what kind of thinking, or what level of thinking, they demand from the reader; whether, for example, the vocabulary is too difficult or the concepts too abstract for those at an early stage of development. Perhaps Rousseau would have had no fault to find with books for children today since so many are beautifully adapted to the child's level and deal with things and situations the child knows, so that the child is in little danger of forming erroneous concepts. This is probably true especially of leisure time books, though school books have also improved. The popularity of Piagetian teaching about stages of development which, as we noted, has some resemblance to Rousseau's, has confirmed teachers' awareness of the need to suit books and other teaching to the stage the child is at. In particular, Piaget's emphasis on the idea that most young people reach the stage of formal operations (coping with abstract ideas) only in adolescence, sometimes in late adolescence, has certainly contributed to simplifying what is taught. Yet simplifying is not enough. Today many critics share Rousseau's concern that children may gain from books prejudices which they are too young to understand but which they simply accept – such things as sexism and racism may be part of the erroneous concepts which children may derive from books.

Freedom in learning

It is probably by introducing various 'freedoms' that child-centred education has most affected the work of schools. Where formerly pupils were expected to remain silent except when replying to the teacher, pupils now can talk with each other during some activities and indeed are positively encouraged to do so in some lessons, provided that the conversation is about the topic being studied. They can usually decide where they will sit in the classroom, though this depends considerably on the teacher's ideas and methods of organising work: and they may move around the classroom without asking permission – though again this depends on the teacher's preferences in classroom organisation. In the early school years children are likely to have freedom to choose which activities to engage in, though choices are inevitably limited by the resources available, e.g. sand, water, clay, paints. These free play periods which are now commonplace in nursery and primary schools sometimes allow the child not only to choose activities but to decide how long to continue with them: but a time limit is usually set to this part of the school day.

Freedom of choice of activities and deciding how long to spend at any one activity is less frequent as the child gets older and especially at the secondary school stage. Possibly the option system in the secondary school curriculum is an attempt to give some freedom to the learner but timetabling complications and pressures to choose according to ability or career intentions rather reduce the amount of true freedom exercised in making these choices. Yet some schools do try to give some time during which pupils engage in freely chosen activities – and of course extra-curricular provisions increase the chances of following individual interests, often for as much time as the individual chooses to give.

THE DALTON PLAN

One method which increases the learner's freedom in some respects is the Dalton Plan, according to which pupils are given assignments which must be completed within a specified period of time (a week, two weeks, or a month) but each individual can choose, on any day, which subjects to work at and how long to give to each. (In the original form of the Plan, pupils signed contracts that they would complete the work in the time specified, thus accepting clear responsibility for their programme.) For example, one day the pupil could go to the mathematics room and spend an hour or more there: then move perhaps to the history room and work for half an hour there: then go to the science lab and work on that assignment for two hours: and so on. In each case the appropriate teacher is present in the room to give advice or help if necessary. The learner thus has freedom to follow up what seems interesting at the moment and is spared the irritating interruptions when bells ring and bring to an end something which is proving really absorbing. The learner can also choose whether to indulge in favourite subjects to begin with or whether to intersperse these with other less attractive work. But of course the method still imposes restrictions on freedom since the assignments have to be completed within the given time and so, eventually, there is a compulsion to do some work whether the learner feels like it or not. Moreover, the content of the assignments has been decided by the teachers, as has the choice of subjects to be studied, even if teachers can devise activities within a given assignment which will allow the pupils some individual choices. The teacher, incidentally, may welcome the freedom given to attend to individual learners in the subject room rather than have to concentrate on a whole class at one time.

This method, including a number of variants of it, has been and is used in schools in many countries with considerable success: yet it has not become widely accepted even though those who have used it agree that it does give pupils a chance to practise organising their own work and discovering how to use such freedom and that pupils generally seem to enjoy and respond well to the method. Perhaps the problem, from the school's point of view, is that it does require considerable planning and organisation to ensure that assignments are appropriate and that pupils are making reasonable progress with them, so that no pupils fail to get through the work in the time available. Progress is usually recorded by a system of column diagrams which show the individual how much has been achieved (this can be motivating) and which show the teacher the stage reached by the class: but these also need careful organisation. There is also the matter of ensuring that resources are available for enough pupils and that the subject rooms are easily accessible: yet these problems are not usually great. Initially, however, the Plan does demand major changes in the school's work and this is probably deterrent, especially as thought has to be given also to deciding whether the whole of the school week is to be spent on Plan work or whether part of it – possibly afternoon sessions – is to be reserved for group lessons. The method therefore seems to recur every now and then under a new name: or individual teachers may decide to use the time allocated to their subject by letting pupils work on the Dalton Plan or some variant, though obviously the amount of freedom thus available to teacher or pupil is considerably less than when the whole school is following the method.

Similarly, in a minor way, the use of study periods or work cards can give pupils a greater degree of freedom. The project method, when it means that pupils decide on a topic or problem which interests them and set out to discover more about it, using a variety of references and methods and, often, devoting a considerable amount of 'free' time to it, is another way in which teachers give greater freedom to the individual learners. The astonishing amount of work which some individuals are happy to do in such circumstances may possibly be regarded as proving that the child-centred educator is right in believing enthusiasm for learning is a natural characteristic of human beings: though the response to the Dalton Plan, project method and other variants, is not always, alas, 100 per cent satisfactory. (But then teachers are scarcely accustomed to 100 per cent success rates in their work.)

EXPRESSIVE ARTS IN THE CURRICULUM

Child-centred views have also affected the school curriculum though these changes may have been so gradual as to be almost imperceptible. Since child-centred educators believe that the individual has the potential to be creative, children have to be given the opportunity to express themselves in various arts. They should not, it is held, be made simply to imitate or reproduce the work of others. Added to this has been a gradual filtering into education of psychological doctrines emphasising the emotional aspects of child development and suggesting that emotional development is aided by expressing emotions through art. For a variety of reasons therefore more space is now given to the expressive arts on the school timetable, though they do tend to vanish as the learners move up in the secondary school. Drawing, painting, crafts of various kinds, music, physical education, dance – all these have achieved greater prominence and are seen as offering possibilities for individual self-expression – though most recently, the emphasis on craft and design technology, while still stressing development of the creative abilities of the individual, has tended to include considerations of practical utility. Within individual subjects there has also been an evident change of emphasis. In the teaching of 'art' there has been the move from accurate drawing of objects, reproduction of 'still life' compositions, to experiment with design, printing in colour, illustrating imaginative themes. In the teaching of 'music' there has been the evolution from 'singing lessons' or formal study of musical compositions to work with different musical instruments, to composing new rhythms and new melodies. In drama, there has been the move from acting the classics to role-playing, to group productions of their own dramatic inventions.

We can perhaps see more clearly how far acceptance of the more child-centred approach has taken place if we recall now the views of the French philosopher Alain (Emile Chartier) who affirmed[9] that psychologists were wrong in seeking to discover in children's drawings the expression of a personality or worthwhile creative achievements. Children, he maintained, are still confused as to what they are trying to express: their drawings simply convey immaturity and lack of skill. By learning the techniques of drawing by copying masterpieces they will learn the skills essential for use when they have matured and have something of importance to express. How many teachers today would unhesitatingly agree with Alain?

Yet in one respect there has already been some indication of a retreat from an earlier child-centred position. In teaching children to write stories or other compositions some teachers have believed that correcting errors of spelling, punctuation or sentence structure would inhibit the child's flow of thought and so prevent the child from being creative. But now there seems to be greater support for the view that attention to correct expression is not damaging – and indeed there seem to be some research findings to this effect. So self-expression without care about the medium of expression is less popular than it was. Some teachers have suggested that a happy compromise can be reached if children compose their statements on a word processor: it is then relatively easy to revise what has been written and make any necessary emendations.

OTHER CURRICULUM CHANGES

Religious education

The question of child-centred education and religion is particularly interesting. As we noted, Rousseau held that the young child is not capable of understanding religious teaching and there-fore such teaching should be postponed to adolescence when the individual's mind has matured sufficiently to be able to cope with these concepts. Later child-centred educators – but by no means all – have expressed similar views and in recent times the studies carried out by Goldman[10] would seem to lend support to this view. There is too some incompatibility between those religions which teach that 'the heart of man is desperately wicked' and the child-centred educator's view that the human being is naturally good. Similarly, the discipline of natural consequences would tend to avoid emotions of guilt, the child following rather a dispassionate course of recognising that some actions are not to be repeated simply because of their consequences. And if the child-centred educator is ready to explain that some 'bad' actions of a child are due only to lack of foresight or immaturity, it would seem inconsistent to encourage the child to repent as religious teachers might think appropriate. Admittedly, if natural conse-quences are extended to include the reactions of other people, the child might then experience feelings of inferiority or guilt, especially if the kind of response chosen by the adult was to exclude the child from the company of others for a time: to indicate disapproval of an action without indicating disapproval of the individual committing the action is rather difficult. So even child-centred educators might produce guilt feelings in the child, even if these would not be based on religious teaching.

But what in fact seems to happen is that child-centred edu-cators introduce the teaching of religion at different stages and in different ways, according to their own religious belief or lack of belief. Rousseau would give, in adolescence, an introduction to a non-specific belief in a benevolent deity. Froebel believed that from an early age the child is aware of the Divine in the created world and can respond to teaching about the Divine creation. Homer Lane, who himself had a strong religious faith, was unhappy that, given the choice, few of his community chose to go to church – but he would not impose church attendance. Neill, similarly, would certainly not have thought of compulsory religious education. Progressive schools which have attempted to put child-centred education into practice have on occasion been accused of being 'godless' but in some instances have presented the pupils with the kind of religious teaching and observances which the school's founders thought right – though again they would not compel pupils to engage in religious observances.

So far as ordinary schools are concerned, we can see changes in thinking over the past decades. The majority of the Plowden Committee, [11] in the 1960s, clearly accepted that children should be given the traditional teaching of religion, even though the main thrust of the Report was to concentrate attention on children and their needs at different stages of development. But since that time schools themselves have in many cases changed the kind of religious education they offer so that instead of teaching with a view to making children believe in the doctrine presented, they now offer rather information about different religions and, in theory at least, leave to the pupils the freedom to choose their own religion. We shall return to this topic of religious education later but the greater attention now given to respecting the individual's right to choose would seem to show a child-centred orientation (even if there is still some tendency to omit consideration of the individual's stage of mental maturity).

Sex education

The spread of sex education in the school curriculum at both primary and secondary levels seems also to owe much to child-centred ideas. Admittedly, sex education may be introduced for utilitarian reasons since the consequences of ignorance may be highly undesirable from the point of view of society as well of the individual. The present campaign concerning AIDS would certainly seem to have such immediate practical concerns in mind. Earlier decisions to give sex education would seem to have arisen from the belief that the child's natural interest in sex organs and in reproduction was to be accepted and responded to. Many child-centred educators, notably Neill, have deplored the bad effects on individuals' emotional development of early training which regarded sex interests as wicked and sought to eliminate or suppress them. Yet the further extension of natural interests to sexual activity in adolescence has provided a problem for various child-centred educators. Neill himself, rather against his will, found it necessary to point out to young people at Summerhill that pregnancies would not be acceptable either within or outside the community, so intercourse should not take place: yet today improved contraception would weaken that argument. The consistent child-centred educator would however argue that the individual who has been well educated should, by adolescence, be accustomed to thinking about consequences and respecting the rights of others and so can be trusted to use whatever information is provided in sex education in a reasonable way. Even so, the individual's judgement as to what is reasonable may not be the judgement of all members of society and parents especially are likely to have strong views on this matter. We shall in fact return to this problem later. Meanwhile we may note that although child-centred views may have helped to establish sex education as part of the curriculum, this still remains an area of much controversy.

SHOULD EDUCATION BE COMPULSORY?

Child-centred ideas have had more impact on education, both in schools and at home, than we normally realise: today many teachers take for granted ideas and attitudes which teachers of earlier generations would not generally have accepted. But a basic question about the child's freedom to develop naturally has not yet been satisfactorily answered. In most countries of the world today children are compelled to receive education, normally by school attendance, and their parents have to see that between certain ages children are being taught. Children really have no choice in the matter, apart from passive resistance. Yet possibly they would choose, if given the opportunity, to spend their time very differently. After all, it is only in the last two centuries that compulsory education has become widespread, if not universal. Formerly children simply took part, according to their competences, in the ordinary life of their parents and the rest of their society: and in some parts of the world they still do this.

Some attempts have been made by child-centred educators to free children from the compulsions of schooling. One of the features which has most impressed people about Neill's school, Summerhill, is that attendance at lessons was not compulsory. If pupils preferred not to learn school subjects but to spend their time in some other way, then they could do so. (Eventually all seem to have decided to attend classes though one girl is reported to have refrained from doing so for three years and the record seems to be held by one boy who stayed away for twelve years.) Of course it may be said that by making classes available and by putting the young people in a situation where most of the peer-group were attending classes, Neill was exerting pressure on them to decide to attend. Certainly Neill himself seems to have regarded it as satisfactory when various individuals finally decided to attend what were, apparently, lessons taught in a fairly traditional style – and this view could be supported by the argument that the desire to learn is indeed natural, even if some bad early experiences of schooling may divert it for some time. At any rate, this was one attempt to respect the individual's freedom of choice. But other educators working within the public system of education cannot leave pupils free to decide whether to come to class or not – Wills recognised this as a handicap in his work in the Barns experiment.

Nevertheless other attempts to reduce the limits on individual freedom were made in the late 1970s when the 'free school' movement brought together in small groups adolescents who had rebelled against attending ordinary schools and offered them a free choice of activities, helped by volunteer teachers. These units do not seem to have survived long though some claimed considerable success during their brief life span. There were perhaps special problems here because the earlier experience of these adolescents had had deep-rooted adverse effects which would have taken a long time to eliminate and which were bound to impress outside observers and even the helpers unfavourably – one such helper recorded that, given the freedom to choose, some adolescents want simply to sit around talking and smoking.

We should remember here that education does not have to take place in schools. In some countries parents have the option of making alternative arrangements, as they have in the United Kingdom. So a parent who holds strong views on being child-centred may free the child from the 'tyranny' of school attendance, even if the parent will still have to produce evidence that the child is receiving a satisfactory education. We shall see in a later chapter the complications which may arise here but it is an interesting possibility for preserving the child's freedom. For teachers in 'ordinary' schools who are strongly child-centred the question of compulsory attendance must remain worrying.

De-schooling

A much more drastic attack on the dominance of the school system was made by Ivan Illich and others in the 1970s. In his book *De-Schooling Society*, Illich proposed[12] that human beings everywhere should be freed from the unreasonable horrors of schools. He criticised the way in which schools formalised knowledge, gave learners the impression that they could learn only through school (whereas, he pointed out, the most useful learning of our lives takes place outside school) and produced feelings of exaggerated respect for school certification of attainment as well as feelings of inferiority among those who were unsuccessful in school work. The cost of school systems in both money and personnel was another reason, though of a different kind and of special importance for Third World countries, for proposing the abolition of the system. In place of schools Illich proposed learning webs, arrangements by which learners would have easy access to the resources they needed to study, not only books but machines and other inventions; a free market by which those with skills they could teach would offer them to those interested; peer-group learning in which people interested in the same topics and skills could meet together to help each other to make progress; and even experts who would be ready to advise and guide those who wanted to learn. Illich and others who joined in this movement apparently believed that human beings do want to learn and that their individual curiosity and energy will lead them to make the kind of effort necessary to seek out information and contact those who can teach the skills they want or who share their learning interests. To this extent the movement could be regarded as sharing some part of the theory of child-centred education, though in other respects it differed from that approach. Illich also seems to have assumed that parents would naturally not inhibit efforts by their children to learn but would support them in their search for education. His view also included the belief that the creative ability natural to humans is inhibited and destroyed in societies dominated by formal, artificial schooling.

Critics of the movement had some faults to find with the proposed alternatives. Peer-group learning already exists, they pointed out, at least for adults who come together in all kinds of organisations – gardeners' associations, music-lovers' societies, pigeon-breeders' societies, for example: but providing access to resources inevitably requires organisation – the bureaucracy so much disliked by the reformers is almost inevitably going to recreate itself. Then, too, the experience of past centuries when it was left to individual parents to make decisions about their children's education and provide for it demonstrates the considerable inequalities which result when such 'freedom' is given. Nevertheless, it is probably significant that very many teachers have been sympathetic to de-schoolers' views. Such teachers themselves have criticised the deadening effects of external examinations, the false importance attached to gaining a 'piece of paper' and the constraints of inert or outdated syllabuses which keep teachers from teaching what they think would be much more valuable and interesting to their pupils. Many teachers and parents note too the apparent loss of enthusiasm and liking for school which too often appears as the young move through the school system. Hence their appreciation of the new perspective on education which the de-schoolers offer.

An equally devastating attack on schooling, and on the child-centred movement itself, came from Philippe Ariès[13] who argued brilliantly in his book, *Centuries of Childhood*, that providing schools for children is not necessarily a step taken in their interest. The alternative view is that by segregating young people in schools adults are barring them from full participation in the real life of society, a participation which children achieved at a fairly early age in past centuries and which the child labourer in some Third World countries today still achieves, even if as an exploited and rather helpless member of society. Various motives can be attributed to adults' willingness to recognise childhood as something separate from adult life. What has been interpreted as an attempt to protect the innocence of childhood by putting children into an environment specially designed for them could also be interpreted as an action which maintains the younger generation in a state of subjection to its elders and postpones the time when it might challenge the power of the elders. Saying that childhood is a distinct and separate stage in development can be a subtle way of excluding the young from participation in adult affairs and sharing in decision-making. This argument is reinforced by observations that conditions in traditional schools can be likened to those prevalent in prisons, since individual freedom of movement is restricted, other people make decisions about the most elementary actions of the individual, conditions are austere, punishment for transgressing the rules is harsh. Granted, these interpretations depend on – one hopes – extreme examples of schools in the past and on an over-generalised statement of what happened to children in them. Yet they do serve to show that in making special provisions for childhood there could be an unintended creation of barriers and some restriction, rather than protection, of the individual's freedom. (Protections allegedly introduced to keep women safe from various dangers may have similar limiting effects.)

THE TEACHER'S ROLE IN CHILD-CENTRED EDUCATION

Possibly one of the major effects of child-centred theory is the change it introduces in concepts of the teacher's role. Traditionally the teacher has been seen as the expert possessing knowledge which is to be passed on to the child. Now it is proposed that the teacher should retire to the background, simply supplying resources the child may need in the process of discovery learning and in following natural interests in learning. From the creative role of 'moulding' the clay into the desired forms, the teacher moves into the apparently less creative role of the gardener. The teacher becomes a 'resource person', possibly joining with the learner in a cooperative exploration of materials and situations on an equal footing.

Providing resources

This reinterpretation leads to several questions and arguments. It is true that children can learn a great deal if given suitable resources and left to get on with it. An early demonstration of this was given by the work of Maria Montessori[14] who was child-centred at least in her belief that the child is keen to learn and is capable of learning independently. She devised 'materials' especially to help young children to learn: for example, to enable them to be independent in dressing themselves she devised frames holding two pieces of cloth which had to be buttoned together – the child could practise with this equipment until the skill of buttoning things together had been acquired. Similarly, playing with boxes containing different substances – gravel, sand, pebbles – could let the child develop better hearing discrimination. And the child could 'learn its letters' by playing with outlines of each letter mounted in sandpaper shapes on cardboard: tracing these shapes (rather uncomfortably, one thinks) the child who also named them could suddenly discover the ability to put them together in a familiar combination of sounds (m–a–m–a) and so spontaneously discover how to read and write. (Quite a number of modern toys for children seem to be derived from the original Montessori materials, even if such materials have been criticised by other educators as not giving the child enough scope to adapt them for the child's own purposes.) But an argument which arises when the teacher is thought of as a resource person is inevitably that the teacher is making the decision as to which resources are useful to the child: thus the teacher is predetermining the child's learning, even if in a less direct way than formerly. And it could well be that by failure to provide some resources – musical instruments, for instance – the teacher may be depriving the child of the chance to develop a natural interest.

Letting children discover for themselves

There is also much controversy as to whether the child really gains by being left to find things out by discovery methods. Here it is pointed out that there is a great deal to discover and that some discoveries have been made by people of really exceptional ability. It seems a waste of the individual's time if the process of learning is not abbreviated by *telling* the child what has been discovered instead of insisting on the child following a long and slow path which may in the end prove not to arrive at the best possible outcome. Further, it has been shown experimentally that naive observers cannot always see what is to be seen: looking at complicated structures, they do need guidance from an expert who can draw their attention to what is important. So for many critics, while the discovery method is worth using sometimes, to let the individual experience the enjoyment of observing and deducing independently, it cannot be used all the time – and it is a matter for expert judgement to decide how much discovery work can be included. Possibly this judgement would also have to take personality differences into account. It has sometimes been suggested that girls, on average, are less enthusiastic than boys about being left to 'discover' various scientific principles: but again, we would have to be better informed about the effects of earlier experience on individual attitudes here.

Controlling the influence of other children

A rather different problem in accepting the child-centred concept of the teacher's role is the influence of other children on the individual child. Gardeners may simply have to see that each plant has a chance to grow freely and is given appropriate nourishment: but teachers have to recognise that children interact with each other. If the teacher should try not to determine too much for the individual, are restrictions to be placed also on the efforts of children to make up the minds and influence the behaviour of their peers? Is the teacher to be someone who intervenes to protect the individual from undesirable influences of the peer-group – or possibly to protect the peer-group from the behaviour of one or other individual? There can indeed be occasions when the teacher's judgement is not that of the peer-group. Wills reports an interesting example of this in the case of a boy whom the others voted to expel from the Barns community. Wills himself felt that the boy had learned sufficiently from the expression of peer-group disapproval to be a reformed character in future: but the peer-group had suffered too much from this boy in the past: so reluctantly Wills accepted their view, in a truly child-centred way – so far as the child group was concerned. It is indeed characteristic of many child-centred educators that they are willing to regard the reactions of the peer-group as part of the process of natural education: but while on many occasions such peer-group judgements prove admirable there do remain other occasions when the teacher may feel that the immaturity of the young group leads to the wrong judgement. There is also the interesting question of how far acceptance of peer-group judgement is compatible with individual freedom – though this may well seem an instance of an inevitable restriction on individual freedom: the human being cannot exist in a social vacuum.

Being neutral

Since human interaction is inevitable, it has also to be considered whether in fact a teacher can be a 'neutral' agent in promoting the individual's development. Even if the teacher is careful not to say anything which might influence the child's decision-making, there are other cues for the child to follow by studying the teacher's appearance, tone of voice, actions. Children are expert in making such interpretations and they are interested in the reactions of the teacher to what they are doing. Inevitably the teacher conveys what seems to be good and what seems to be bad, from the teacher's point of view. Neutrality is impossible.

Finally it can be argued that in deciding to teach, we have

taken the decision to intervene in someone else's life, to a greater or lesser extent. However much we may respect the freedom of the learner or try to adapt to the learner's abilities and interests, we must make value judgements as to whether learning is taking place satisfactorily. Even if we believe that human nature is innately good and that teaching has mainly to allow natural development, we still have to decide whether the learner is apparently following what we believe is the natural and good course of development. We do know what we expect the end-result to be: and if it does not seem to be forthcoming, then we feel we must intervene. Hence the difficulty of accepting the strict interpretation of the teacher's role as remaining in the background and simply providing resources. Yet it is good to be reminded to intervene with caution.

DOES CHILD-CENTRED EDUCATION WORK?

It is difficult to judge whether indeed child-centred education produces the required and desired effects when put into practice. One reason for this difficulty is that, according to some judges, child-centred education has not really been tried in practice.

It is of course true that many individuals have given child-centred education to a child or group of children and these efforts have achieved some success. Various 'progressive' schools in different countries claim excellent results. Yet it can often be argued that they are in some respects not fully child-centred: and the really important evidence would come from the application of child-centred methods in the ordinary schools of a country, teaching children from a variety of home backgrounds in normal circumstances.

There have been indications in official documents that the schools in England should be child-centred in their work. The Plowden Committee Report, in the 1960s, indicated by its title, *Children and Their Primary Schools*, that the schools were the children's schools but it remains doubtful whether all the recommendations of the Reports were implemented. More recently, the DES, in its guidelines for local authorities[15] entitled *The School Curriculum*, seemed to indicate by the wording of given aims a decidedly child-centred view; in five out of six cases the aim was 'to help pupils to' develop certain characteristics and skills: such wording would seem to assume that the child has already the ability and the interest which would lead to such development. Oddly enough the aim which proposed rather to 'instil' something in the child was the aim of developing respect for others' way of life.

But the mass media have frequently produced the impression

that schools today are, if anything, excessively child-centred in their absence of discipline and neglect of teaching of the basic skills – and this impression is at times unfortunately reinforced by the utterances of politicians. It is therefore useful to have some research which gives a more reliable picture of what is happening in classrooms. A particularly interesting report was given in Neville Bennett's book,[16] *Teaching Styles and Pupil Progress*, which reported a study of teachers' methods and their apparent relationship with pupils' achievement in subjects of the primary school curriculum. What emerged very clearly from that report was that it is very difficult to classify teachers as 'traditional' or 'progressive' in approach since the majority of teachers show a mixture of tendencies. The criteria used to decide whether teachers' work was progressive or not were these:

'1. Integrated subject matter.
2. Teacher as guide to educational experiences.
3. Active pupil role.
4. Pupils participate in curriculum planning.
5. Learning predominantly by discovery techniques.
6. External rewards and punishments not necessary, i.e. intrinsic motivation.
7. Not too concerned with conventional academic standards.
8. Little testing.
9. Accent on cooperative group work.
10. Teaching not confined to classroom base.
11. Accent on creative expression.'

This is perhaps one of the most useful interpretations available of ways in which principles of child-centred education can be translated into ordinary classroom practice, though 'accent on cooperative group work' would not be found in all child-centred theories. But although some rough classifications of groups were made, ranging from the 'traditional' to the 'progressive', teachers whose style could be described as purely in one or the other category were rare. Certainly the general impression was that child-centred teaching is much less prevalent than the media had suggested.

Consequently no very reliable answers emerged to the possibly naive question: 'Which methods gain better results?' In so far as could be judged, data seemed to show that children's achievement was better under more formal or 'mixed' teaching styles – though the apparently most successful individual teacher was 'progressive' – but much also depended on the ability level and personality of different pupils. It was also noted that attitudes towards school tended to improve under an informal style of teaching – but anxiety scores also rose here. Possibly with some surprise it was discovered that in imaginative writing children brought up under the more formal style of teaching did not have lower scores, on impression marking, than those taught in a more permissive way: their results seemed 'to indicate that it is possible to achieve grammatical accuracy without detriment to creative output'.

Other researches in the primary and early secondary school similarly suggest that the teaching styles found in schools today cannot be exclusively classified as progressive or traditional but are rather a mixture which depends on the individual teacher's own personality and preferences as well as the characteristics of the lesson and the general conditions and regulations of the school. Thus Eggleston and Galton[17] classified three teaching styles in science: the problem-solvers, the informers and the enquirers. Enquirers and problem-solvers (if the pupils perceive the problem as interesting them) could presumably be regarded as child-centred. In primary schools Galton classifed[18] teacher types as individual monitors, class enquirers, group instructors and style changers. Again, one can see how some of these might be regarded as child-centred, particularly, perhaps , the individual monitors: but it is notable that here also teachers were observed to employ different approaches at different times. (There may also be differences associated with the age and experience of the individual teacher.) Thus no one dominating technique seems to be evident in either primary or secondary schools: mixtures of methods are found, though the evidence does seem to suggest that in the secondary school the less formal and more child-centred approaches are less frequent.

CONCLUSIONS

At present there is obviously not enough empirical evidence to show whether the child-centred theory of education works. We must also recognise that empirical evidence which simply showed the success of pupils in gaining good results in formal school exams would not necessarily be conclusive. The aim of child-centred education is not really to ensure exam success, it is to help the individual to learn what is useful to the individual and of value: it is also to develop the individual's ability to learn independently, to enjoy learning and to continue to learn throughout life. While success in school exams may be related to some of these characteristics, it is by no means reliable evidence that they are present. We would need wider information here as well as information about the individual's ability to behave well towards other people – and about the individual's happiness or otherwise.

There is too the recurrent question of whether child-centred education really has been put into practice. Some studies have found that some teachers engage in 'token' observance of child-centred methods, for example, assuming that if children are allowed to sit where they choose, to move freely about the class-room, to talk to each other, this is child-centred education – and other parts of the school work can be firmly traditional and formal. In such cases, the theory is not really being used or tested properly. There remains also the very large question whether the compulsion to be educated destroys the freedom of the indi-vidual: yet here it is also argued that naturally the child shows a wish to learn about society and about the natural world, so there is no real coercion in providing education which responds to this wish, merely a fostering of the child's natural growth.

Above all, there is the question whether we can accept the belief that the natural tendencies of the human being are good and that natural interests in learning and in being creative will suffice to produce the well-educated individual, provided that educators attend to these natural impulses and supply a good environment and adequate resources to satisfy them. This is something which cannot be proved. If children are observed to behave badly – badly on criteria accepted by everyone – there is always the argument that their natural goodness has been corrupted by the influence of those around them, or by bad education. Likewise if they fail to show interest in learning, this can be attributed to discouragement in the earlier stages – or even to failure of the parents to foster the baby's first exploratory impulses and responses. It is indeed a matter of faith.

Whatever our response to that essential question, we have to recognise that educators holding a firm belief in the natural good-ness of human beings have carried out excellent work in helping some people who have become maladjusted or delinquent to achieve a better way of behaving and living. We recognise too that changes which have, in a rather erratic fashion, entered into school work as a result of child-centred views do seem to have been advantageous in many respects. (We must of course also recognise that we ourselves may be biased in our judgement here simply because we have absorbed, without recognising them, some of the child-centred principles.)

The question then remains whether education would be improved by a stronger acceptance of child-centred methods, if not necessarily of the basic child-centred principles. Could many people have had a happier childhood and a happier adult life if they had been taught in a child-centred way? Does education in its customary forms bring the young into 'shades of the prison-house'? To find answers to these questions it is necessary to consider, as we shall do in following chapters, the alternative theories and modes of action.

Questions

1. Consider your own education in: (a) primary school; (b) secondary school; (c) college, polytechnic or university. In what respects, if any, was the influence of child-centred views evident?

2. Looking at Bennett's list of characteristics of progressive teaching, indicate which principle of child-centred education seems to be related to each of them.

3. What are the advantages and disadvantages of discipline by natural consequences?

4. Is compulsory education a denial of individual freedom?

5. Has child-centred education good methods to offer even for those who do not accept its principles?

6. Do you feel that your own education failed to develop fully all your abilities? If so, what were the reasons for this failure?

7. What considerations lead you to believe that children are, or are not, naturally good?

CHAPTER 3

Education and society

Child-centred educators foster the development of the individual. They believe that the individual should enjoy education, finding it a source of happiness and fulfilment-discovering and satisfying new interests. They do recognise that the individual has to learn to live with other people and they have often used the influence of the group to help the individual towards development as a good human being: but their interest is focused on the individual child. Is this emphasis wrong? Is it more important to educate children to be good members of society? Would everyone be happier if that happened? The educational theories we have now to consider begin from the principle that education must produce good members of society.

There are obvious reasons for emphasising membership of society. To survive, human beings depend on the help of others: the child especially depends on others for food, warmth, shelter. Communication is necessary to human life: the child has to learn from others how to use language. Beyond immediate communication, human beings also benefit from communications transmitted over long distances of space or time, from the accumulated experience of the human race. Human personality is formed in interaction with others and to express that personality the individual needs a social group. The individual's own contribution to the group or society is minute in comparison with the knowledge and skills the group already possesses, yet the group also needs the contribution of its new members. Hence the need to educate so that the child profits by what other human beings have to offer and in turn contributes to the well-being of society.

Of course much depends on what we mean by 'society'. The word can refer to a small or large group or even to the human race as a whole: it can refer to a national group, to a town or village group or to some impermanent, informal group of people. Individuals can thus be members of various 'societies', some societies being sub-sections of a larger society. Education as a member of society is usually interpreted as preparing for membership of a regional group (village or town) or a national group, only rarely is it for membership of world society. Much depends on what kind of society and what size of society educators have in mind but the focus here is on the needs and well-being of society rather than on individual needs and interests – though it can be argued that the two are not incompatible but, rather, complementary.

EDUCATION IN PRIMITIVE SOCIETIES

Primitive societies are unlikely to question the need to prepare children to be good members of the group. In various parts of the world and at various times in history it has been taken for granted that the children must acquire the group's skills by observing and working with adults and must also learn to live according to the group's customs. The child goes along with the adult on fishing trips, for example. and gradually becomes expert: or the child is given simple tasks, looking for food, carrying water, caring for animals, or, later, cooking and making clothes or tools and so acquires adult skills. Where the society has sex-differentiated roles, boys learn from men, girls from women. There may be formal ceremonies to teach the beliefs of the group concerning the supernatural, or to teach taboos or to recognise a new social status. But education is largely acquired by living in the society and there is little likelihood that the individual will be encouraged to develop different skills and interests from the rest: it would in fact be difficult to do so. The individual's feeling of identity depends on the group's allocation of a role and self-esteem again depends on group approval or disapproval. It has indeed been asserted that in some tribal societies the individual does not have a concept of separate identity but thinks of himself/herself only as part of the group.

As societies acquire more sophisticated skills and books are introduced, this straightforward process of education ceases to be sufficient. The skill of reading may require special instructors as may the teaching of specialised crafts or other languages. As the amount and complexity of knowledge grow, parents or other adults in the child's immediate environment are unlikely to be able to cope with all education so they may group together to hire a tutor, as parents in farming communities have done for some time in different countries. Gradually there is a move to having education provided by groups formally representing the community – by local government councils, by church parish councils or similar bodies – who see to the hiring of teachers and to the conditions in which the children are taught.

CHURCHES AND EDUCATION

In European history church organisations have played a major part in organising and providing education for different communities. In early times, the provision may have been mainly to educate for church service; but both Protestant and Catholic churches later found it appropriate to establish schools to give at least an elementary education to children generally. (In Protestant communities the spread of elementary education was certainly also motivated by the view that individual ability to read the Bible was essential to good understanding of religion.) In some places the state government took over the responsibility for education, but still in accordance with church doctrines. Church education however probably had two aims: the salvation and well-being of the individual and also the creation of good members of the Church – and so of good members of society. We can see this dual aim in statements made by the Protestant Reformers in Scotland in the sixteenth century.[1] In *The First Book of Discipline* they stated that parents should not be allowed to treat their children 'at their own fantasy' as they had formerly done but the parents must be 'admonished and by the censure of the Church compelled to send their children to school so that the commonweal may have some profit by them'. It was a long time before this proposal for compulsory education for all children was implemented in Scotland but it is fascinating to see this early statement of the view that the education of children is for the benefit of the community as a whole.

SPARTAN EDUCATION

But we can find education to be a good member of society flourishing much earlier than the sixteenth century. In Sparta, some five centuries before the Christian era, there was a most radical development of the principle of society-centred education. The Spartan child, from birth, had to develop the characteristics which would maintain Spartan dominance of the country, keeping subservient a slave population, and ready to defend the Spartan state effectively in war. There was indeed an important selection test: babies who were physically deformed or weak were left out in the open to die (a custom not unknown in other societies then and since): such babies, it was believed, could not possibly become useful members of the Spartan group. There was also some sex differentiation since boys were taken from their homes at the age of seven, to be educated in groups, under the supervision of young and adult men. But for all children their purpose in life was clear: they must maintain Spartan supremacy and must not allow their personal feelings to interfere with the well-being of the state. (This principle is illustrated in the legendary farewell of the Spartan women to their menfolk going into battle – 'Come with shield or on it' – that is, come back victorious, carrying your shield, or come back dead, carried on your shield.) Girls were educated to be good wives and mothers for Spartan warriors. Boys were trained to be expert in military skills and to endure hardship uncomplainingly. (The Spartan custom of bathing in cold water can be regarded as having begun a long tradition in education, one which has lasted, in English public schools, right up to recent years.) An important element in Spartan education, we are told, was awareness of supervision by society as a whole and of public approval or disapproval. Any Spartan adult had the duty of checking bad behaviour in any child. Group discussions during the boys' education told of heroic deeds and indicated the virtues and duties to be cultivated. Loyalty to the state was the major virtue: education developed this as well as the characteristics and skills necessary for the well-being of the state.

At this distance in time it is hard to know how effective this early practice of society-centred education was. Certainly Plato[2] found elements in it which he thought worth introducing into his own scheme for an ideal education, outlined in *The Republic*. Others have questioned whether it did in fact produce as much military efficiency as was once believed or whether the Spartans simply were earlier interested in military efficiency than their neighbours, concentrated more on it and so had an initial advantage. It has also been suggested that when they were removed from the immediate influence of the Spartan group, individual Spartans abandoned their homeland principles of behaviour and adopted the way of life – however reprehensible – that they found in their new environment. Nevertheless, the tradition of Spartan education has greatly influenced later educators.

CONTROVERSY ABOUT STATE CONTROL OF EDUCATION

It was many centuries before the idea of national or state control of the education of all children became widely accepted. The churches in European and other countries did make great efforts to provide some form of education for all children. Local communities, through their town councils or other bodies, often also made some kind of provision but in all cases much depended on the home circumstances of the children and the attitudes of their parents towards education. By the nineteenth century it seemed apparent that these voluntary and irregularly available resources were not enough. The growth of industrialisation meant not only the need for education in new techniques but also a redistribution of population so that the demands on the parish organisation became excessive – and churches were also weakened by schisms and loss of public support. There was, too, some concern that the increase in the amount of easily available printed material, books, journals, pamphlets, might spread subversive ideas among the population if education did not ensure the right attitudes among future citizens. Hence many European countries moved towards state or national control of education.

The movement towards intervention by national governments in education was not without opposition. In England especially it was argued – and has been argued since – that voluntary provision and private enterprise were in fact providing some sort of education for practically all children and no interference was needed to ensure that all children would eventually be provided for. Non-intervention, to some critics, seemed much better than invoking centralised control.

The relevant arguments were rather well summarised[3] by Herbert Spencer, writing in the mid-nineteenth century. Governments, he argued, can scarcely be regarded as competent to judge what constitutes a good education. They are most likely to think that a good education is simply like the education they themselves have received – yet that education may have been highly traditional and unsatisfactory. Governments also are likely to think an education is good if it produces citizens who will conform to the existing state of affairs and maintain the existing government in office. So governments are likely to promote an education which will 'mould' good citizens according to the government's definition. Further, although many people argued that more education would lead to less crime in society, Spencer made the point that lack of education is not necessarily a cause of criminal behaviour: the two might be related only because both were associated with poverty. To assume that cognitive education leads to more virtuous behaviour is demonstrably absurd. If, Spencer argued, centuries of teaching by the churches, with the threat of hell for wrong-doers, have not 'sufficed to make men good', how can we expect the admonitions of school teachers, who have no such supernatural penalties at their disposal, to be more effective?

Perhaps more importantly, for Spencer, the intervention of public authorities to provide education was an interference with a natural process of evolution. This evolution is based on a most important factor, the natural tendency of parents to provide for the well-being of their offspring. He noted rather acidly the pride parents take in the 'phenomenal' achievements of their children and pointed out that parents may feel their own well-being in old age will depend on how good an education their children have had. Why interfere with such a strong natural impulse which will ensure that parents provide for the education of their children?

Making such provision is good for the character of parents, since they may have to deprive themselves of some pleasures to do so. They may also give serious thought to the number of children they should have, if they are to be responsible for educating them. If it is argued that parents may not be able to judge well what a good education is, then, Spencer suggested, rather unkindly, they can always ask the advice of experts – and cost is often a good criterion. He believed indeed that people do not greatly value what they get for nothing. (This point seems highly relevant in arguments today – is the public education service under-valued because it is, apparently, free?)

DEVELOPMENTS OF NATIONAL CONTROL OF EDUCATION

In the event, some compromises were arrived at in most countries. The place of the churches was recognised in various ways, either by provision for church representatives on national bodies concerned with education or by approved arrangements for the teaching of religion in public schools. Some countries, like France, attempted to make the public schools of the country secular and leave religion to teaching outside the school: but even here a dual system persisted, church schools continuing to exist alongside the state system. In England also church schools continued to exist, with, through succeeding decades, varying amounts of public financing. In Scotland, by a settlement in 1918, local authorities took over church schools, with safeguards for the continued teaching of religion in these schools according to the original church authority and for the appointment of teachers of the appropriate religious beliefs. (The teaching of religion is something to which we must return in a later chapter.)

Another modification of central control was a division of authority between central and local government in Britain (and in other countries) so that while legal requirements were determined centrally and much financing came from central government, local authorities could also introduce some bye-laws and were responsible, in accordance with central regulations, for some financing of educational provisions. (Appointments of teachers also were not centrally determined in Britain but made at local level.) Thus it could be argued that central control was not absolute in various national systems. Opportunities were given for expression of opinion at local level: and the views of church authorities were still given some place.

In Britain too there was an absence of centralisation of the curriculum. Spencer had pointed out, quite effectively, that it is indeed difficult to decide which subjects of study a government should insist on providing in its schools. Certainly there followed a long period of decision-making and changes of policy about what should be offered at elementary and secondary levels. More importantly perhaps, there was no central policy as to the civic education of the children. Government officials, politicians and others were clearly aware of the desirability of producing good citizens through the education system but, to judge by statements made in the Code for Use in Public Elementary Schools (1904–1926), and subsequently reproduced[4] in the Board of Education's *Handbook of Suggestions for Teachers* in 1937, children were expected to develop the qualities of a good citizen mainly by learning from the example of the teacher and from the whole ethos of the school, in the playground as well as in the classroom. 'Though their opportunities are but brief, the teachers can yet do much to lay the foundations of conduct. They can endeavour, by example and influence. . . to implant in the children habits of industry, self-control, and courageous perseverance in the face of difficulties; they can teach them to reverence what is noble, to be ready for self-sacrifice, and to strive their utmost after purity and truth; they can foster a strong sense of duty. . .' Further, the school, in cooperation with parents, was 'to enable the children not merely to reach their full development as individuals, but also to become upright and useful members of the community in which they live, and worthy sons and daughters of the country to which they belong'. Possibly it was also assumed that the teaching of religion in schools would do much for the moral, and therefore the civic, development of children. It is interesting to note that in France, where religion had been excluded from the curriculum of the public schools, there was introduced the teaching of 'morale', lessons advocating the development of various individual and civic virtues. But in France as in some other national systems there was probably a rather greater emphasis on ensuring that the schools produced good and loyal citizens.

THE SCHOOL AND SOCIETY

The introduction of national education and central government control did not have the far-reaching effects – at least initially – that some people had feared and others had hoped for. Although many countries were concerned to produce good citizens and although they were also concerned, it was said, to develop the technical skills necessary in industrialised societies, schools did tend to focus on cognitive developments, teaching the three Rs, certainly, and in addition giving some kind of general or liberal education. Admittedly, of course, other aspects of school life – assemblies, pictures, flags, extra-mural activities – could be regarded as contributing to civic education. All the same, the concept of the 'fortress school' as a place where children were separated from the normal life of society, and possibly protected from some of the stresses of society, seems to have prevailed in many countries during the nineteenth and twentieth centuries. So, too, the focus on developing the individual's abilities remained, even if it was asserted that the individual owed service to society.

DEWEY AND EDUCATION FOR SOCIETY

The educational writings of John Dewey[5] offered a different and stimulating view of the school's functions. He emphasised the importance of society for the individual and the need to learn through communication with other people. Schools should therefore have a special relationship with the society around them. The school should simplify the knowledge and customs of society so that the learner can understand them better: it should purify these, introducing to learners only those elements of society which are worth transmitting (the criteria here were not entirely clear, though presumably the teachers had to judge): it should balance impulses from society, preventing the child from being too strongly affected by one particular part of society.

It concerned Dewey that schools failed to provide children with knowledge of some essential skills which formerly they would have learned in their home surroundings, the skills of producing food, clothing, warmth. Hence his Laboratory School in Chicago in the last decade of the nineteenth century gave children the chance to acquire these skills: and indeed, since Dewey also held that most human beings are 'hand-minded', interested in learning through practical activities rather than through words or books, these seemed particularly good studies.

Dewey argued further that some choices of subjects to be studied in school, and the customary exclusion of some other subjects, are due to unthinking retention of values held by societies in the past. The respect given to 'liberal' subjects in the curriculum and the low esteem accorded to technical and applied subjects seemed to him relics of past social structures where these subjects had been associated with superior or inferior social classes. In classical Greek society, for instance, philosophy and allied subjects had been the preserve of the free citizens who did not need to work for a living while the crafts had been the study of the artisans, socially inferior people. Similarly, 'culture' had come to be regarded as the property of a small social elite. He proposed a considerable re-evaluation of subjects, getting away from the traditional view that some subjects have peculiar merits and are bound to produce certain changes in the learners. The study of a subject has merit only if it *does* produce desirable changes, i.e. if it interests the learner, proves useful to the learner in attaining the learner's purposes and leaves the learner ready for further growth and learning. According to Dewey these results were more likely to occur, for most people, if some practical activities were involved: and it was essential that the learner should be interested in the study. (Hence the development by Dewey's followers of the Project Method which does indeed focus on the wish of the individual to find out more about something or to solve some problem. The individual becomes aware of a problem, to construct, improve, enjoy something, and plans how to solve it: the individual then carries out the plan: then evaluates the solution – was the plan good? Could better action have been taken? And this method can of course also be used by groups of people.)

Since Dewey's emphasis on interest has led to misinterpretations of his theory and to accusations that he introduced 'soft pedagogy', pandering to children's whims, rewarding them without cause and trying at all costs to keep them 'happy', it is important to note his interpretation of 'interest'. This interest should not be of a fleeting, superficial kind and it should not be an interest in acquiring extrinsic rewards. People should work because they perceive that what they are doing is important to them, because it helps to solve their problems, to give them information and skills which they see as useful. This kind of interest indeed will keep children working (and adults) even when the going is tough: it produces the kind of self-discipline necessary for effective learning and eventual success. (He recognised that some forms of manual work, e.g. in factory production, are by no means interesting or stimulating to the intelligence; they can be acceptable only in so far as the individual worker is aware of a wider purpose of the activity in contributing to the good of society.)

Dewey's emphasis on interest and his attack on the excessive reverence paid to the traditional book-learning also led to some charges of being anti-intellectual. But it is abundantly clear that a major aim in education as he understood it is to cultivate the individual's intelligence, to make the individual think. He differed, however, from child-centred views like those of Rousseau in the importance he attached to the influence of the social environment and in his assertion that individual abilities do not simply develop, their development depends on the way in which they are used and the social circumstances surrounding the individual. Education, in his view, prepares the individual to live in society through living in society. But at the same time it fosters the individual's own interests and independence of judgement. Individuality and living in society were not incompatible in Dewey's view since he had in mind preparation to live in a democratic society: and a democratic society, in his interpretation, is one which allows the individual to think and judge freely and respects individual differences in interests and abilities. It is also a society which communicates freely with other societies and in which there are no hard barriers between groups inside the society.

Dewey's theory of education could thus be interpreted as a kind of middle position between the theory that education must develop the individual and the theory that education must develop good members of society. It is dependent on his view of the 'democratic' society. Not all societies which claim to be democratic would have the characteristics he expected.

In practice, as we have noted, the development of central control by a government representing society has varied considerably in different countries. The limits set on that national control in various systems indicate possible uncertainties about the desirability of taking away from those who formerly were in control – the family, the local councils, the churches – some rights to decide what is to happen in education. While it can be argued that these groups are able still to influence central government since their members join in electing it, there still seems to be a belief that they represent special interests within society which might otherwise be overlooked. The limits set indicate also, perhaps, less than complete acceptance of the view that education should prepare individuals to be good members of society: they result, possibly, from some belief in the importance of concentrating on the education of individuals. Other systems of education, however, show a more complete acceptance of education for society and assume that all groups share the same principles and have the same interests. We have therefore to consider these other interpretations of education for life in a democracy.

COLLECTIVE EDUCATION

What is a collective?

The theory of education which determines education in many parts of the world today is that of collective education. This theory emphasises that the individual is to be educated in and by society to become a good member of society and work for the good of that society.

The word 'collective' is relatively new in discussions of education but it is increasingly often used. It can be used either as a noun or an adjective. It refers to a group of human beings united by some common purpose which they jointly try to achieve. Some collectives are short-lived, some last for months or years, some continue indefinitely. A film society, for example, can unite people with a common interest in films for months or years before, for various reasons – loss of interest, change of membership – it becomes ineffectual and ceases to exist. A cricket club or tennis club similarly can have a life-time of many or only a few years. But while the collective lasts, its members recognise that they have a purpose in common and they are willing to make efforts, to a greater or lesser extent, to ensure that the group achieves this purpose. They may adopt a distinctive form of dress or badges to make recognition of fellow-members easier and to proclaim the existence and importance of the group. More permanent collectives may be found in church organisations. A long-surviving example may be seen in religious orders where those having a common religious purpose have lived in a community, subscribed to its rules and worn a distinctive dress or emblems. The individual's views in such a case are clearly subordinate to the rules of the community as a whole, while the community as a whole is subordinate to the wider rulings of the order and of the church to which the members belong. Churches themselves can be regarded as collectives, international collectives comprising the church's adherents in different countries, or national collectives, the church membership within a country. They too have ceremonies and emblems which mark membership of the group and reinforce statements of the group's purposes and beliefs. In this example one can see how there can be smaller collectives, possibly with rather different activities, within a major collective but all sharing the purpose of the major collective.

Individuals in modern society may belong to a number of collectives, at work or during leisure. The school itself is a collective, if all those working in it – pupils, teachers, other staff – are aware of its main purpose and willing to do what they can to ensure that that purpose is achieved. Within the school, the individual class can be a collective, if teacher and pupils are concerned to promote the learning and happiness of the group; the school sports teams can be smaller collectives as can the school orchestra or choir or school societies. Individuals can thus be members of minor collectives within the larger collective though all would have in common the well-being and progress of the people in the school. Unfortunately, there can be opposing collectives within a school: there can be a collective of the staff and a collective of pupils who have different purposes. Some pupils in the school may also have no sense of belonging to a collective, either the general collective of the school, or the class collective or a school society or team collective. Some of course may belong to collectives outside the school – to a neighbourhood youth club or sports club or church organisations, or to a neighbourhood gang. Others may be solitary individuals.

The family is the first and most frequently experienced collective. Families normally have a common purpose, the well-being of their members individually and collectively, though the strength and extent of that purpose varies greatly. In some circumstances it may be a matter of simple survival, trying to keep everyone fed, clothed, sheltered. In more affluent societies, this kind of common purpose may be less apparent and a strong force for the unity of the collective is removed, though families may still be united by determination to maintain the standard of living already reached and by the desire to promote the happiness and success of all the family. Of course in some families the collective spirit is non-existent: individuals are concerned only with their own well-being and feel no responsibility to contribute to the common well-being of the household. Similarly, the size of the family collective may vary from the nuclear to the extended family. Many critics have deplored the disappearance of the former loyalties of the extended family, a disappearance more apparent in some regions of the country than in others, and perhaps more frequently observed in Western societies than in others.

The purposes of the family collective may conflict with those of the larger collectives since promoting individual well-being may in some interpretations lead to selfish behaviour and disregard for the well-being of others. Loyalties may differ if, for example, a family seeks to protect one member from the consequences of breaking a law. This danger is widely recognised in any large collective and indeed Plato tried to avoid it in his ideal state by proposing that the Guardians, the philosopher-rulers, should not know which were their own children, the children being brought up communally. In this way, he hoped, the situation would be avoided in which those in positions of authority favour their own kith and kin by giving them positions for which they may not really be well qualified. He also hoped that the normal feelings of family loyalty might thus be extended to all the children of a given generation. Other schemes for collective education have their own ways of avoiding possible dangers from family loyalties, though ideally there should be no conflict between the purposes of the family and those of society in general.

Collective education in the Israeli kibbutz

Probably the best example of collective education today is found in the Israeli kibbutz system. The kibbutz was first introduced in the late nineteenth century as a self-supporting settlement of Jews in Palestine: with the establishment and growth of the state of Israel such units have increased and developed. In principle the kibbutz is a self-supporting and largely self-sufficient community originally agricultural in nature and, in early times as well as in some regions today, having to be ready to face attack from opponents of the Jews. Early settlements therefore found it useful to gather babies and children together in houses built specially for them, thus relieving their parents of the day-to-day tasks of child-care and enabling them to devote their time and energies to the work of the kibbutz.

Present-day kibbutzim vary in their religious or political orientation: essentially there are three major groupings of kibbutzim. The guiding ideology ranges from strictly orthodox Jewish to different forms of communism. Kibbutzim also vary in size, from a few hundred to some thousands of members. They further vary in the strictness with which collective life is interpreted for children. In the strictest form, the babies go to the babies' house from birth or from the age of one or two days: there they are cared for, the mother visiting to feed the baby and both mother and father coming to be with the child at various times. The babies and older children are cared for by people designated for this work by the kibbutz as a whole. As the children grow older they may move to a house for pre-school children, then to the children's house, then to the house for adolescents: the number of sub-divisions depends on the numbers in the community. As the children reach school age, schooling is provided for them, using the same curriculum as schools outside the kibbutz (it must be recalled that the kibbutzim population accounts for only 5–6 per cent of the population of Israel). If the kibbutz is too small to provide adequately for secondary education, the adolescents may travel to a neighbouring kibbutz to share in its educational facilities. As they grow up, the children continue to visit their parents in the parents' own individual house or are visited by them. In recent times, there have been increases in some kibbutzim in the number of occasions on which children can stay overnight in their parents' house. They may also meet their parents during regular work hours, depending on what the parents' occupations are, especially as, when they grow older, adolescents must give some hours each week to work in the kibbutz.

It is abundantly clear to children growing up in this kind of society that they depend for everything not on their parents but on the efforts of the whole group. Food, clothing, shelter, education – all come from communal resources. From these also come companionship and affection, for although close links with the parents can be maintained and are maintained, yet for much of the time the individual is in the company of the peer-group and grows to rely on their support and their approval or disapproval of individual behaviour. In later adolescence, the decision whether the young person is to receive higher education again depends not on the individual or the parents but on the kibbutz. If it seems that the higher education of the individual would be of benefit to the community generally, then the kibbutz may decide to support the individual through such studies. In other cases the decision may be that this would not be a good use of the collective's resources.

Many studies have been made of the kind of personality this system develops and of its general effectiveness. Much seems to depend on the orientation of the researcher. Against the system it has been argued that parents, mothers especially, may feel deprived of their children's affection and regret not having closer contact with them. Jealousy may even develop if the woman who cares for the babies seems more important in the child's life than the mother herself. Parents may feel powerless to intervene when the community makes a decision regarding their child which they themselves do not like: and children, in some cases, may feel alienated from their parents because they are not there when needed or they prove unable to help. On the other hand it is pointed out that much may depend on whether the parents are first-generation members of a kibbutz or second generation. Those who have been brought up under the kibbutz system will have different expectations of the relationships between parents and children. They may have liberated themselves from the cloying closeness and possessiveness of traditional family life.

So far as personality types are concerned, it has been argued that the system produces confident, loyal members both of the kibbutz and the greater Israeli state. It is noted that kibbutzim have produced a greater proportion of political leaders and eminent members of the armed forces than would be expected from their actual numbers. Against this, other observers suggest that there is also produced an assertive, abrasive, somewhat insensitive personality: and that kibbutzniks tend to be limited in outlook, concerned with the affairs of their own community but not with wider national or international concerns (which is an attitude not unknown in the products of other educational systems). It has been suggested too that the people raised in the kibbutz find it difficult to adjust to life outside and to cope with separation from the peer-group on whose presence and support they rely.

Clearly it is unsatisfactory to over-generalise and assume that all those educated in a kibbutz conform to one type. Possibly an indication of the satisfactoriness of the system might be found in the ratio of adolescents who apply to be members of their kibbutz when they reach the appropriate age. Here, 'holding power' varies from one kibbutz to another: overall, certainly more than half opt to stay in the system but an estimate of 90 per cent remaining is probably rather high. Reasons for not applying for membership – or not being given membership – vary considerably.

The size of the Israeli kibbutz clearly gives some advantages in educating children to be good members of a community by living in that community. Even in the larger kibbutzim, the dependence of the individual on the work and the judgement of others can be readily perceived and standards of behaviour are common to all children and reinforced both by adult and peer-group opinion. The processes of collective decision-making can also be learned by observation and experience, though this becomes rather more difficult as the size of the kibbutz increases – and also, perhaps, when the kibbutz engages in industrial work as well as agricultural or horticultural or even employs outside workers.

Certainly the process of collective education becomes more complicated in societies where the traditional family unit still remains and where very much larger numbers and greater varieties of work are present. Loyalty to the Israeli kibbutz may also have been strengthened by the threat of attack from outside, so perhaps one cannot easily generalise from this example.

Large-scale collective education

Collective education takes place in many other countries today – in the USSR, the Soviet bloc countries, in China and in some African states. It can be said to take place in Japan in certain respects[6] for although the Japanese believe that the child is born good, they also consider it important to train the child from the beginning in how to behave towards other people, how to observe the customs of society. Situations are avoided which would make the baby cry or cause unhappiness: but there is constant teaching and reminding about what is to be done or said in social situations. There is also encouragement of the child to be cooperative and friendly towards other people. The child is taught to 'be like other people' by acquiring the correct forms of behaviour, speech, and attitudes. The family collective is very strong and plays a great part in this education though neighbours and pre-school teachers make an important contribution. Later in life many Japanese (males, at least) will find themselves part of a work collective in industry or commerce where group loyalty and cooperation are again strongly emphasised. Yet in the process of formal schooling, individual ambition to succeed is of major importance. On the national level, the aftermath of the war and the discrediting of the imperialistic attitudes of that time have made the teaching of patriotism less certain and school policies in this respect have been and are still the subject of controversy. Nevertheless considerable emphasis on belonging to the national collective remains.

Possibly the most obvious examples of large-scale collective education today are to be seen in the Soviet Union and the German Democratic Republic. Much of the theoretical basis for collective education there came from the work of A. S. Makarenko, a much-respected educator of the Soviet system.[7] He was responsible, after the Revolution, for teaching a group of homeless and semi-delinquent youths, developing them into what was eventually known as the Gorky Colony. Later he was similarly responsible for a larger group of adolescents, working in factories but living in a community, the Dzerzhinski Commune. In his autobiographical account, *The Road to Life*, Makarenko tells how he initially tried to use with these difficult young people the child-centred pedagogical training he had received in the years before the First World War: but he found their laziness and insolence intolerable – they were prepared to let the adults do all the work but showed these adults no respect or even courtesy. At a crucial point Makarenko lost his temper and insisted that the youths follow his instructions and get on with the work essential for the continued survival of the whole community. Under his firm direction, the group, motivated initially by the simple need to have shelter, warmth, enough to eat (conditions in those post-revolutionary years were difficult), gradually developed its own form of self-discipline and its own rules. From these and other experiences Makarenko worked out a theory of education explained both in his autobiographical account and in *Problems of Soviet School Education*. We find there the importance attached to the group's discussion of the behaviour of its individual members as well as the importance for the group of having its own self-respect and standards of achievement. There is thus pressure on the individual to live up to the group's ideals.

Yet Makarenko was not proposing that the group should be left to arrive unaided at its decisions. On one occasion, we learn, he deliberately prevented the group from discussing and judging one youth whom he suspected of having stolen. Here he thought the individual could reform if given a second chance but he did not think the group would see the situation in this way. (This contrasts interestingly with Wills' acceptance of the group decision in a similar situation.) But Makarenko was well aware of the care that the leader must take when individual wishes and aptitudes are concerned. He tells also of a boy who was unusually gifted as an actor but who, like many boys at the time, thought he wanted to train as an engineer. In this instance Makarenko brought the question to the attention of the group who decided that the boy must give up his technological studies and go to a theatre training school instead. Since the boy depended on the collective for a maintenance grant, he had to accept the group decision: and eventually he became a most successful actor and was grateful for the earlier compulsion. Yet Makarenko was uncertain, later, as to whether he should have intervened. He decided that in education 'there must be a general programme, a pattern, and also an individual amendment to it.' He had no choice as to whether he should educate all his pupils to have certain characteristics – 'to grow up a brave, staunch, honest and industrious patriot'. But possibly individuals should have free choice in developing their aptitudes and choosing a career. The general responsibility of a teacher in a collective remains clear nevertheless. As Makarenko put it: 'I am profoundly convinced that every teacher will be confronted by this question – has he the right to interfere in the development of a character and guide it in the correct direction, or must he passively look on? To my mind, the question should be answered in the affirmative – yes, he has that right.'

What are the methods used to produce the good collective and the good member of a collective? Considerable importance is attached to membership of youth organisations. In the Soviet Union pre-school children and young school children are members of the Little Octobrist movement (so called in memory of the October Revolution). This is mainly an organisation which provides social events and parties on important days – 1 January or May Day for example. It does begin some teaching about the ideals of Lenin and it makes children aware of belonging to a larger society.

More important is the following youth organisation, the Pioneers, which children belong to between the ages of, approximately, seven and fourteen. Each school has its Pioneer room, for meetings and other activities. Teachers are specially trained to be Pioneer leaders. When children reach the appropriate stage, they are ceremonially welcomed into membership by older Pioneers. The movement has its own newspaper, *Pioneer Pravda*, and it organises study circles in out-of-school time, and holiday camps. In larger centres of population there will be the Pioneer Palace – which may be literally a former palace – in which special facilities for all kinds of leisure activities are provided, e.g. for chess, photography, model-making, sewing and embroidery, sports. The uniform is simple – a badge and red neck scarf – added to the still customary school uniform. Yet any child not wearing it would feel conspicuous in a class where everyone else is doing so. Pioneers are given very clear rules of behaviour (and schools also have explicit though brief statements of what is expected of pupils) and each Pioneer group has the duty of observing how each of its members behaves. If anyone is behaving badly or failing to do school work well, he or she will be called to account by the group and exhorted by the group or its leaders to reform. It is of course also the duty of individual Pioneers to notice the behaviour of their friends and to help them to behave well and work well. This also is made very clear to Pioneers.

Later, the Soviet adolescent can become a member of the Komsomol, the League of Soviet Youth. Not all adolescents become members: the more enthusiastic and socially active young people join, with, possibly, some hopes of progressing eventually to membership of the Communist Party. Komsomols also have group meetings and clearly stated duties. They are expected to act as models of good behaviour and to try to raise the standards of behaviour and political understanding among their peers. At university or other institutions of higher learning, the Komsomols have responsibility for such practical matters as maintaining cleanliness and tidiness in student residences as well as for encouraging social activities and participation in political discussions or manifestations.

Similarly, in East Germany the Young Pioneer and Ernst Thälmann Pioneers provide the same kinds of social education, study circles, leisure-time activities. At older age levels, the Freie Deutsche Jugend (Free German Youth) organisation has much the same purposes as the Komsomols.

East Germany has also had, since 1954, an interesting Youth Consecration (Jugendweihe) ceremony for those at the 14-year-old stage. Young people are prepared for this ceremony by special teaching during the school year leading up to it, e.g. they may hear talks by outside speakers – politicians or skilled workers – and visit places of historical or civic interest. On the appointed day parents are invited to the ceremony at which, during a programme with musical interludes, there are speeches by a distinguished Party member, representatives of the FDJ, and teachers: and the young people respond 'Yes, that we solemnly promise!' to questions whether they are ready (1) to join with the older citizens in protecting the 'great and noble cause of socialism' and 'the revolutionary heritage of the people'; (2) to work hard towards, and in, further education (including both culture and trade skills) and 'to devote all your knowledge and skill to the realisation of our great humanistic ideals'; (3) 'always to act in comradely cooperation, mutual respect and helpfulness, and always to associate your own way to personal happiness with the struggle for the happiness of the people'; (4) to work for friendship with the Soviet Union, peace, and the cause of inter-national socialism.[8] They shake hands with the visiting speaker and are presented with an appropriate book; and members of the Pioneer group give them flowers. The occasion is further marked by family parties and presents – department stores have counters showing suitable gifts for the occasion. Clearly the intention is to mark the acceptance of the young person into the adult community and to emphasise to the young people the duties of that membership though, with the higher school leaving age at 16, the ceremony seems now to come at the wrong age level. But again the collective education system gives an explicit statement of what is expected of citizens and asks for a public commitment to living up to these expectations.

Collective membership and public approval or disapproval may also be made more obvious in other parts of the educational system, in holiday camps or in work experience. In both the USSR and the GDR the inclusion of work experience in the school timetable is to give not only practical skills but also an awareness of the contribution of such work to the well-being of society and the importance of each individual's satisfactory performance. In work situations too there are Boards of Honour showing the names or photographs of those who have done particularly good work – as there are similar Boards in schools. Again, members of the work group have a responsibility for criticising, where appropriate, the performance of their peers and seeking to help them to do better. (Such responsibilities may also extend outside the work situation, if, for example, a fellow-worker is having marriage problems or failing to ensure that his/her children attend school regularly then help and counselling should be given by others in the group.)

Pre-school education may both reinforce the feeling of group membership and reduce the force of family influences for in these systems extensive provision is made for both creches and kinder-gartens. In the USSR the availability of places for pre-school chil-dren depends on the geographical region but in the GDR some 60 per cent of children aged from 3 months to 3 years go to creches and over 90 per cent of those from 3 to 6 years attend kindergartens (some of which can be weekly kindergartens, the children going home only at week-ends). And once the children are at primary school there is a further provision of supervision and activities in the school after school hours so that, if the family so chooses, children are looked after until their parents can collect them after work. These provisions naturally contribute to enabling women to work outside the home, so they have clear utilitarian value. But they are also regarded as important forms of education, even if the importance of the home is stressed and contact between school and home prescribed and cultivated.

At the end of compulsory schooling there is the question of vocational choices and vocational training. While the freedom of the individual to make such choices is recognised, collective education for membership of the larger collective of society as a whole does introduce some additional considerations. Attempts are made, by manpower planning, to decide what the needs of society are for qualified people in the various kinds of work. Places in vocational training centres and in institutions of higher education are adjusted in numbers to correspond to the expected needs of the economy. Consequently the child moving through school is likely to be made aware of what possibilities there are and is counselled by teachers as to the direction which might best be followed. Similarly, for entry to higher education, candidates may find strong competition for some branches of study and demands for not only a good academic record but also a good record of social behaviour if a place is to be granted. In some cases candidates may have to show seriousness of purpose by working in the economy, in a suitable occupation, for some months or a year or two. While maintenance grants are given when the candidate has achieved a place, failure to study adequately means loss of grant – and probably of the place. Further, since the number of places has been calculated on the basis of society's needs, changing from one line of study to another may be impossible: if the choice has been mistaken it may still be necessary to complete the full course and work in the occupation for a given period until application can be made for further studies. (It should admittedly be kept in mind that evening study may offer an alternative if a place has not been found in full-time education or if the present occupation proves uncongenial.)

A corollary of the support given to students or apprentices during their training is that the collective is entitled to their work in an appropriate post once they have qualified. Graduates, for instance, are sent to their first job and expected to remain there for at least some years. They can, of course, bring to the attention of the appointing authorities circumstances which would make a certain posting reasonable or otherwise (marriage, for example): and it is reported that some ingenuity is shown here. But their obligation to the collective is again clearly stated. (It is difficult to predict what may be the results in a collective system if the unemployment crisis affecting many countries at present spreads and the collective finds that it does not in fact need the work of all its members. Admittedly, jobs of a token kind might be created to spare individuals the humiliation of being apparently not needed: or perhaps, in centralised systems, job-sharing could be more generally organised. It remains to be seen how the economic systems of collective economies develop and how they can react to changing and possibly decreasing demands on a country's work force.)

The teacher's role in collective education

A major point in teaching in a collective educational system is that the teacher speaks with the authority of the whole collective. The teacher has learned the ideals of the collective (and presumably accepts them) and knows that these ideals and the behaviours they imply must be developed in the new generation. Therefore, in dealing with parents or children, the teacher is in no doubt as to what is right: and parents and children know that the teacher is right in representing the views of society. It is not a matter of arguing about individual preferences.

Similarly the teacher is sure of carrying out a social duty in educating the children to accept the norms of society. While collectives may well accept adult debate and criticisms about the ways in which the collective's principles are being put into action, there is certainty about the principles and purposes of the collective and the young have to learn these.

The teacher knows that his or her role is not simply to provide for cognitive learning but to attend also to personality development. (Books in different subject areas will probably combine factual information with the collective's interpretations of history, geography and other studies, and indeed literature may be chosen to offer, in the actions of its heroes, moral teaching about how to behave and how to think about life.) The characteristics to be developed are clearly stated – the good member of the collective will be loyal, hard-working, cheerful, resolute, cooperative, unselfish, capable of self-criticism, devoted to promoting the common good. The teacher should of course give an example of such characteristics in the teacher's own behaviour.

The teacher should cultivate the development of a good collective spirit in the class or work group.

The teacher should maintain close contact with the pupils' parents, visiting them at home as well as meeting them on formal occasions organised by the school.

The teacher should take part in extra-curricular activities and help children's study circles. (As part of their training, student-teachers in the GDR have, in addition to ordinary teaching practice, 'social practicals', which mean work during some weeks in Pioneer or other extra-curricular activities.)

The teacher should also take part in other social and political activities.

EVALUATIONS

These ideas form the theoretical bases of collective education. As always it is difficult to be certain how fully they are applied and how much success they have, especially as they are used in so many different countries, each of which may introduce variants or be affected by different historical, economic or geographical circumstances. (It has to be recalled that the political philosophies of countries using collective education can also vary greatly.)

We can see that the system in different places does succeed to some extent in producing individual citizens who are indeed loyal, hardworking and enthusiastic: but to judge of the average attitude is more difficult, especially as communication with other systems may be officially controlled. No system, so far as one can judge, is perfectly successful. It is evident from educational journals within the Soviet system, for example, that not all schools function as intended, that not all teachers are truly conscientious (some, for instance, may give pupils higher marks than they deserve because the true mark would not look good for the reputation of the teacher or the school) and that many people are more concerned with getting a comfortable job and relative riches for themselves than with working for the common good. We can see also, in some countries, relatively high rates of alcoholism, which would suggest that life in the collective (as in other forms of society) is not wholly satisfactory. On another level, it can be argued that the continuing interest in religion in some countries where, theoretically, it should have yielded to devotion to socialism, suggests that the collective kind of education has not provided a satisfactory purpose in life or a satisfactory interpretation of life. Family ties also seem to remain of major importance for many people and often supersede those of loyalty to the larger collective.

At the same time we can see in Western democracies indications of interest in collective education and some use of its methods. The use of school uniform to denote group membership and produce feelings of loyalty is traditional in many countries even if it is now being replaced by an 'informal uniform' dictated by the preferences of the peer-group. Similarly, various games have been regarded as valuable in fostering the team spirit, the willingness of the individual to be cooperative and to sacrifice personal glory for the good of the team. House systems in various schools have been intended to promote these feelings of loyalty and concern for the well-being of the collective. The English 'public schools' have in many ways exemplified collective education, including the forms of social control exercised by the peer-group. Yet the norms accepted in the school or house or team collective have not necessarily been identical with those of the wider collective, society outside the school. And while it could be said that such schools try to foster ideals of service to the larger collective in adult life, they also certainly promote personal ambition. They would consider that their purpose is to ensure the best possible development of the individual rather than to produce a loyal, unselfish, good member of a given society, though they might argue that the two are not incompatible.

There is evidence that educators in some Western democracies feel that their system is deficient because it does not produce in most young people feelings of concern for the rest of society and of membership in the larger society. Many young people, it is claimed, feel no responsibility for the well-being even of their immediate community. Individualism has been over-emphasised.

We find such criticisms, among others, in David Hargreaves' book,[9] *The Challenge for the Comprehensive School*. Here he suggested that many pupils emerge from the school system alienated from society in general, partly because the school fails to provide teaching in accordance with their real interests. The curriculum should therefore be amended to include community studies and practical activities which might serve to build up links with the rest of society and produce feelings of 'social solidarity'.

Similar concerns were evident in a Report of an Advisory Council for Education in Denmark, proposing a better educational system for the 1990s (the *U 90* Report).[10] The school must not only prepare future citizens by providing good vocational education and language skills, it must also develop a good understanding of the political system of the country in the past and the present, and in comparison with systems in other countries. Moreover it must 'try to imprint a positive attitude to the basic principles of our version of representative government'. This seemed possible since some 'concepts and legal provisions are so fundamental that most people in society will as a matter of fact accept them, and it is necessary that the next generation have a positive attitude to these rules implanted at an early age'. Moreover the school must teach such principles even if some parents would not accept all of them. The school, according to the Council, cannot remain neutral: parents' prejudices should not remain unchallenged even if the parents disapprove of the school's teaching. And while it is recognised that the young must be encouraged to think for themselves and make their own decisions, they should do so on the foundation of learning about the basic principles. Schools should avoid the development in young people of purely negative critical attitudes: automatic negation is as irrational as unthinking acceptance of the existing state of affairs.

In many respects this seemed like a prescription for collective education in a Western democracy. But the Report also revealed the problems of trying to define the ideals of such a collective. Already the published document included a number of minority statements dissenting from those of the majority, some of these on important principles, others on relatively minor points. The main text itself shows the difficulty of reaching agreement about those fundamental principles which are to be instilled. It suggests that some values change in the course of time: so it seems that some values might be rejected or discarded. Further, it considers that some values may be characteristic of different social classes, listing those more likely to characterise the working class (e.g. group solidarity) and the middle class (e.g. thrift). Hence we remain uncertain whether in fact there is enough general acceptance of common principles to make for really effective collective education.

Similar uncertainties emerge when we think of the possible development of collective education in other Western democracies. There are long traditions of rhetoric about the importance of developing the individual as well as serious concerns about the dangers of unchecked centralised control of education. Then, too, the idea of patriotism has fallen into disuse, if not into disrepute, in various places in recent times – it depends, of course, on how patriotism is defined. In England, notably, all that seems to be offered in proposals for teacher education[11] is that teachers should know 'ways in which pupils can be helped to acquire an understanding of the values of a free society and its economic and other foundations'. It is a mild and mainly cognitive proposal, especially in comparison with statements in collectively oriented educational systems.

Yet the difficulty of defining agreed principles and educating children to accept them and act on them is obvious. In many societies today we find considerable regional as well as social class differences in defining values which should be passed on to children. Different religious beliefs also mean differences of values – as does the absence of religious belief or vague retention of some religious teachings. Multi-cultural societies, by definition, must have different principles and ways of life which various groups want to pass on to their children. In such cases, is there sufficient common ground to make collective education possible? Educational systems must, in such cases, reflect thoughtfully as to which principles could be generally agreed – and which beliefs might be regarded as parental prejudices which the school must challenge.

Despite such complications, we can distinguish in the theory of collective education many positive advantages. It offers clear guidelines as to the purposes of schools and of society. It gives the individual the reassurance of peer-group companionship and acceptance and clear standards of behaviour. Teachers work also with clear guidelines as to purposes and with the full support of the rest of society for what they are trying to achieve. The common purposes and common curriculum of schools may well facilitate movement of teachers or pupils to different areas: and more efficient provision of resources may be a side-effect. Parents also have guidance and support in bringing their children up to be good members of society.

Development of individual aptitudes and interests may also be fostered in collective education since such development can benefit all society. Indeed, individuals may profit by greater support than in other societies when they seem to have worth-while gifts to cultivate. But of course social support is unlikely for individuals whose work in science or arts or other spheres is deviant and appears unlikely to help the collective. They may then suffer also social disapproval.

Critical judgement also is encouraged in some respects in collective education. But limits are set to its exercise. The norms of the collective remain paramount and the maintenance of the collective is essential. Again, deviance beyond the tolerated limits will evoke collective social disapproval: and within the collective society the deviant individual is unlikely to find the refuge available in some other societies, membership of sub-groups which share the individual's deviant views. Individuals too may question whether life spent in the service of the collective is wholly satisfying to the human being, even if this service is interpreted as working for the good of other humans.

Altogether, the theory of collective education offers much of value but raises many questions of principle and practice. It is in fact probably easier to apply in small groups: but education cannot forget about the larger society. So is a move towards collective education desirable?

Questions

1. Which methods of collective education are used with children and young people in our society? How effective do they seem to be?

2. What are probable merits and weaknesses of the Youth Consecration ceremony?

3. What advantages may be claimed for bringing children up in the peer-group rather than in the family unit?

4. Was Dewey over-optimistic in claiming that education for society also allows free development of individual thought and aptitudes?

5. To what extent have Spencer's arguments against government control of education been justified by later experience?

6. Does Makarenko seem to have been right in judging by his experience that child-centred educational principles are invalid?

7. Should fees be paid for higher education? Should students receive full maintenance grants or be helped by loans which are to be repaid later? Should graduates be directed to work in appropriate posts?

8. How attractive is the role of the teacher in collective education?

9. What conflicts of principles among different groups can be observed in Western societies today? Do these conflicts make collective education impossible?

CHAPTER 4

Rights and responsibilities of parents

Parents have a headstart in educating children. Their behaviour, from the earliest days of the child's life, influences and teaches. They continue to be educators, in some sense, so long as the child or young person is living with them. From parents, the child learns to use words, to dress, to behave in certain ways, to eat certain foods: the child also acquires, uncritically, mannerisms and attitudes – sometimes to the astonishment of rather embarrassed parents. Other influences soon become effective, especially those of siblings: but siblings themselves have been affected by parents' behaviour. It is particularly worth noting, in societies where the ideal of equal opportunity is emphasised, that parents are, in many ways, the strongest force against equal opportunities. For the child, much depends on whether parents provide good examples, create a loving environment in which the child has ample opportunities to learn, take thought for the child's education and well-being. Even when children enter into the formal system of education, these parental influences remain effective. Parents provide different environments and different kinds of care for their children. The only way therefore to secure complete equality of opportunity would be to remove children from their parents' care and bring them up communally. (And even then the transmission of hereditary factors of health and physique would remain.) Few educational reformers have been willing to propose quite such a drastic reorganisation of society though some societies stress communal activities to an extent which may reduce parents' influence. If we value equality of opportunity, we must consider this question: how can education give all children the opportunities which are afforded by good parents, and avoid or eliminate the bad effects of some parents' rearing of their children? And, another major and related question, for what reasons should other people, or the agents of society, interfere with the educational provision which parents choose to make for their children?

We must not assume that all children are brought up in what we tend to think of as the typical family unit of a father and a mother and one or more children. In present-day Britain,[1] for example, some 916,000 children are brought up in one-parent families, either because they are the children of single mothers or because they have lost one parent by divorce or by death. In America, in 1979,[2] of children under the age of 18, 16.9 per cent lived with their mothers only, and 1.6 per cent with fathers only. Absence of the support normally given by the father or the mother may cause problems, even if, in the traditional family, mothers and fathers are not always good role models nor agreed about their policies. In addition to these and to financial difficulties, much depends naturally on the extent to which society in general expects males and females to adopt different patterns of behaviour and interest. While the problems of the single mother have received quite a lot of attention, the problems of the single father, unaccustomed to domestic chores, inhibited in buying clothes for a young daughter, for example, have only recently received attention. The situation of children living with step-parents and half-brothers or sisters is another variant of the traditional pattern, bringing its own complications. A relatively new and infrequent pattern is that of child-rearing by lesbian or male homosexual couples.

Nevertheless it is generally assumed that parents – biological, adoptive, legally united or otherwise – provide for the material needs of children and have a strong emotional attachment to them. In fact the great majority of parents do have ambitions for their children and hope to see them achieve a good standard of living, probably rather better than that of their parents, in a safe and harmonious world. Consequently, parents are taken to have the right to make decisions about the kind of education their children will receive since they are doing so much to protect and care for the children. These rights are forfeited if the parents are judged by other people to be acting in a way which is bad for the child or bad for the rest of society. The principle is simple; but its interpretation and implementation prove complicated. What problems arise in limiting parents' care for their children?

LIMITATIONS ON PARENTS' RIGHTS

The reduction of parent power from the classical *patria potestas* which gave the father the power to decide whether the child lived or died has been a matter of slow evolution in different countries during many centuries. In the nineteenth century there still remained the view that the father could dispose largely in matters affecting the child's health or possessions. It is relatively recently that legislation has provided for removal of the child from the parents' care if physical injury to the child is being inflicted, or if the child's physical health is threatened by the conditions parents provide. Similarly, if the moral well-being of the

child seems in danger because of the home conditions or the behaviour of the parents, again social agencies can remove the
child from the parent's care. These are matters of welfare legislation rather than of educational but they do have clear relevance to the child's capacity to benefit by education. What is
noteworthy is that there is great reluctance on the part of many
social agencies to take such steps: great importance is still given
to the emotional attachments which the child may have even for
cruel or immoral parents. The recent investigations of baby-
battering and the sexual abuse of children show not only that
some parents do not provide for their children as is traditionally
expected but that, to a great extent, members of society, in an
official capacity or as individuals, are reluctant to intervene in
family situations: many babies, children and young people have
continued to suffer because of some people's belief that a 'real'
parent is better in any case than a substitute parent or than in-
stitutional care.

COMPULSORY EDUCATION

As we saw in Chapter Three, legislation to make education
compulsory for all children between certain age levels has been
regarded by some critics as a massive denial by society of the
right of individual parents to decide how much, if any, education
their children should receive. (The Islamic Republic of Iran still
refuses to make education compulsory since it is unwilling to
compel its citizens to send their children to school.[3]) Intervention
is in most countries justified on the grounds that it safeguards the
rights of children, since some parents demonstrably have in the
past provided very slightly or not at all for children's education.
In some instances parents have regarded the child's work as
important to the family and therefore resented the time taken
from that work by educational requirements. (In rural areas there
have been in the past – and still are – periods of absence from
school at harvest time: and girls everywhere remain in danger of
being kept at home to attend to domestic work or child-care. In
some Third World countries where education is not compulsory
for all children, such factors may prevent many children from
attending school. Indeed, an educational project in a district of
India found that to reach children it was helpful to provide
evening classes which they could attend after the day's work was
over.) But the intervention in Western societies to make
education compulsory has also been justified on the grounds that
a society today needs citizens who have received at least a basic
education and, in many cases, some vocational preparation in
work skills. Thus, to benefit both children and society parents do

not have a choice, where children in designated age groups are concerned: such children must be educated. In many cases too the amount of work that children may do during hours when they are not at school is restricted by legislation; though this does not really affect work done without pay within family concerns.

Parents however may still have some choice as to how the child is to be educated. While there is legal provision that children must receive an adequate education, it is possible for parents in the United Kingdom and some other countries to make their own arrangements for that education and so avoid having to send their children to school. They then have to convince the representatives of society that the education they are providing is satisfactory: judges in these cases will be officials or inspectors of the local government – or, ultimately, of national government. Parents' reasons for taking this kind of action vary greatly. In some cases they believe that the public school system is not providing a good enough education or that it offers an irrelevant education: alternatively, they may consider that the local school to which their children would have to go does not offer a good environment for their children. Parents then may decide to educate their children themselves, using their own knowledge and skills: or they may join with other like-minded parents to make informal group arrangements to educate a number of children. Convincing the representatives of society that these alternatives are satisfactory is possibly easier in systems where the public school timetable and norms of achievement are not sharply defined: it is then harder to prove that the child's progress is not up to standard. Much also depends on whether the parents themselves seem competent as substitute teachers: professional teachers have obvious advantages here, though it might be asked why they do not send their children into the system in which they themselves work or have worked. Similarly, the qualifications of people specially hired by parents to teach their children are also to be carefully scrutinised.

Curiously enough, in recent cases in Britain where parents' provision at home for their children's education has been challenged, the arguments have tended to bear upon the social aspects of education (the children are said to be missing the companionship of other children in school) rather than upon the cognitive. This growing emphasis on the social or emotional aspects of education is evident also in the criticisms sometimes voiced against parents who have provided special tuition for their children in, e.g. mathematics, music, sport. In these cases some critics argue that the children must miss the normal social growth which is said to come from learning in the peer-group: there is an unexamined assumption that all must pass through the same learning experiences, preferably at the same rate, so that all grow up in the same way, avoiding any specially high levels of achievement. Granted, history offers some striking examples of parents who did give their children an unusual or remarkably rigorous training: but it is doubtful if subjecting them to the common education of their time would have been an ideal alternative. (Montaigne's father, we are told, made it easy for his son to learn Latin by ensuring that all those tending the baby and young child used Latin in speaking to him: the method apparently worked very well until the father lost confidence and sent the boy to an ordinary college.)

For whatever reasons, there has recently been an apparent increase in the numbers of parents preferring to make special provision for their children's education. The movement Education Otherwise has recruited many parents in the United States and Britain who want to opt out of the public system and provide what they consider to be a better education. In exchanging information and ideas, such parents find themselves encouraged and helped. Yet some questions as to the supply of equipment and the use of suitable teaching methods must remain: provision is probably easier at the primary levels, so far as resources are concerned. Professional teachers may well wonder how efficiently untrained parents can teach, even if they have the advantage of small groups – and some special claims to attention. Here, on the other hand, we might recall another argument of the philosopher Alain, that parents are naturally bad teachers of their children.[4] Too much emotion comes into the situation, he affirmed. Parents are too easily irritated if the child does not learn rapidly and well: they project themselves into the child's performance and lose their temper if the work is not of a high standard (just as, possibly, husbands are not good at teaching their wives to drive). On the other hand, parents may yield to emotional appeals by the child to take things more easily, may accept a slapdash performance, or agree to stop and do something more agreeable, whereas the impersonal discipline of the school day teaches the child that there are rules about time which have to be observed. It is an important part of learning for the child to discover that the child's own blandishments may have no effect on a teacher who has to deal with other children and other problems, and that personal charm and affection do not compensate for unsatisfactory work.

It is of course true that there are circumstances in which parents, whether naturally good teachers or not, have to cope with teaching their own children. If the family is living in a foreign country where schools use an unfamiliar language or are inappropriate, or non-existent, or if the family lives in a sparsely populated area, as, for example, in some parts of Australia, then unless the child is to be sent away to a residential school, parents have to teach as well as they can. In such circumstances parents have been helped by organisations like the Parents National Educational Union, which earlier provided correspondence course materials for families living abroad and which still provides such courses for parents teaching their children at home. Such arrangements as the radio broadcasts for Australian districts where children are widely separated from other children offer another possibility. There are also many commercial producers now offering to parents books and materials which will enable them to teach their children (possibly more often in the earlier years), and so substitute for what schools offer, or supplement schools' work or, as teachers may at times feel, provide a competitive and contradictory version of the school curriculum.

Nevertheless, in many countries of the world today parents have clearly lost the right to decide how many years of their children's lives are to be given to the process of education. This limitation has been imposed by societies to safeguard children and, to varying extents, to benefit society. Some critics might argue that state intervention has not gone far enough in this respect since the willingness, or ability, of parents to maintain and pay fees for their offspring still affects greatly the amount of education received. Some parents provide for additional teaching during the years of compulsory education, either in school subjects or in some not included in the school curriculum: or they provide pre-school education where the public system does not begin till the age of 5, 6 or 7. Some continue to support their children into higher education, higher degree courses or further vocational training. Such differences are not always a matter of the parents' financial resources, though obviously low incomes set limits to what can be done and increase the keenness of both parents and children to reach the time when the children can add to the family income. But while compulsory education can be interpreted as an attempt to protect the rights of children and society, it can also be judged an incomplete attempt: possibly more intervention in the form of student maintenance grants and abolition of tuition fees in higher and vocational education is required for adequate safeguarding of children's rights – though such measures, as we have noted, eventually involve judgement as to how much the individual then owes to society and as to how that debt is to be paid. Parents are perhaps more generous than society in thinking about such debts.

FURTHER LIMITATIONS ON PARENTS' FREEDOM

Within the provisions made for compulsory education there are various factors about which parents have little choice. It is true that legislation in Britain, as in other countries, has stated that parents' wishes are to be taken into account when schooling is provided. But this good general principle becomes difficult to interpret in practice, especially when it is associated with the other legislative principle that this provision must not lead to 'unreasonable' public expenditure. The judgement as to what is reasonable tends to be left to local education authorities, though an appeal to central government is possible – if parents know about and exercise their rights. We find therefore that sometimes parents do succeed in having fees for special kinds of tuition paid by the local authority for their children, if the local authority does not itself offer that kind of teaching in its schools – fees, for example, for attendance at schools specialising in music or ballet; or some parents may make a case that their child needs the benefits of a residential school. Such provision by local authorities is obviously likely to suffer in times of economic crisis: but it also depends greatly on the educational views of the local authority. Some local authority views on education give parents greater freedom than others: yet local authorities are presumably all agents of the same society.

In various major instances parents have found that local authority policy means that parents' wishes respecting their children's education cannot be freely followed: e.g. parents preferring single-sex education in a local authority area where coeducation is the chosen policy may have no possibility of getting their children to a single-sex school, unless they leave the public sector. Muslim groups in some areas of Britain have recently shown their unwillingness to send their daughters to local authority coeducational schools, but without effecting a change of policy. Similarly, a group of parents who argued that they wished to have selective secondary education rather than comprehensive schools for their children found on appeal to central government that these wishes also were not supported by the official interpretation of the Education Act. Yet in some areas, other groups have fought successfully against local authority plans to restructure some existing comprehensive schools or against proposals to abolish existing secondary schools: it is also proposed in England that concerned parent groups should unite in protest if a new government tries to abolish the few (175) remaining grammar schools. Certainly parent groups sometimes succeed – according to the area or parliamentary constituency in which they live perhaps – in preventing closure of a local school. Such instances bring to attention not only the apparent arbitrariness of constraints on parents' choice of schools but also the greater effectiveness of parent groups, rather than individuals, in trying to affect policies.

Individual parents have also, on various occasions, found that because of zoning regulations they cannot send their children to their preferred school, preference sometimes being based on family tradition, sometimes on convenience of access, sometimes on judgement of the goodness or badness of a neighbourhood school. Whether parents were able successfully to change the original allocation of their children to a certain school depended in the past all too often on the willingness of local authority employees to admit that this could be done, the meek or ignorant parent probably accepting resignedly an unsatisfactory allocation. More recently, the Parents' Charter in Britain, and governmental emphasis on parents' rights, have meant that parents are given more choice and are made aware of their freedom to choose. Many authorities pride themselves on the fact that almost all parents do get their children into the preferred school. But the obverse of this new freedom for parents may be difficulties for society's representatives in schools and administration. If a school gets a bad reputation, deservedly or otherwise, or if it is rumoured that the school is to be restructured (to lose, perhaps, some of its year-groups) or even to be closed down, there may be a flight of parents (and children) so that the numbers in the school are sharply reduced: staffing is then adjusted and so the various rumours become a kind of self-fulfilling prophecy. In the same way, schools may suffer from an excess of popularity as large numbers of parents apply to have their children admitted. Legislation in Britain now protects public finances by providing that the school can refuse excess numbers or applicants whose needs would lead to demands for resources (of staff, subjects, accommodation) which the school does not have.

THE USE OF CORPORAL PUNISHMENT IN SCHOOLS

A considerable problem for parents may be the punishments used in the school the children attend. For example, corporal punishment has produced disagreement between schools in Britain and parents in two ways. Some parents who do not themselves approve of such punishment have objected when their child is subject to it. Some parents who do approve of it and use this method themselves consider that the school should be using it, though it has been abolished. Internationally we find that many countries have abolished this form of punishment in their schools and they consider countries still using it as barbaric. In recent years, some British parents have complained to the European Court of Justice against the infliction of corporal punishment on their children at school and judgement has been given that this punishment constituted a violation of human rights, since it was contrary to the philosophical views of the parents. Consequently there were some proposals in Britain that schools should in this matter accept the parents' philosophical preference, so that some children whose parents approved of corporal punishment should continue to be subject to it while those whose parents disapprove should be exempt from it. This would have produced a really remarkable example of careful respect for parents' rights of choice – and after all, school teachers' behaviour in punishing and supervising children has been assessed or justified until now by reference to their status of being *in loco parentis*. But it was not a workable solution in the ordinary classroom situation and now corporal punishment has been eliminated in the public school systems. Some after-effects remain: e.g. in 1987 the European Human Rights Commission awarded damages of £3,200 to a young man who, in 1982, had refused to accept caning after a fight in class – his father had supported him in this refusal and the young man was suspended from school until he reached school-leaving age six months later. (We must remember society's possible sanction in such cases: if parents refuse to send a child to school because the parents disapprove of the school rules or discipline, they may be charged with failing to fulfil the legal requirement to have their children educated: this sanction is occasionally used though normally efforts are made to resolve such conflicts in other ways.)

In the movement to abolish corporal punishment it seems as if decisions have not much been related to the views and rights of the other parties concerned. Teachers' responses vary: some teachers welcome the abolition of a method they themselves do not use or wish to use: others regarded this method as useful as an immediate sanction in difficult circumstances and feel that alternative sanctions ought to have been made more readily available – such sanctions as suspension from school tend, they argue, to take much time and paper-work and eventually prove ineffectual. In addition to such practical considerations, some teachers judge the method as incompatible or compatible with their child-centred views or their determination to make pupils good members of society. Pupils' views (in systems like that of Scotland where, until very recently, corporal punishment was used) have also proved mixed. There has usually been a sex difference since girls apparently are more sensitive to the public disgrace of the method: but a substantial number of both boys and girls have indicated that they find this kind of punishment acceptable, particularly if it keeps under control pupils who would otherwise disrupt the work of the class.

It remains unclear whether the abolition of corporal punishment in schools results from a spread of child-centred views or not: references to parents' rather than children's rights to decide school policies make such interpretation doubtful, though again it would be argued that parents in some social classes today are indeed more child-centred in their views. The present attitudes could be due rather to the principle stated[5] by the Roman educator Quintilian in the first century of the Christian era that such punishment, besides being ineffectual, is unsuited to free human beings – 'fit only for slaves'.

It is also unclear whether the actions and protests of some groups of parents reflect the opinion of the whole population or whether the views of the British Parliament are not in accord with those of the majority in society – such divergences can occur. It would seem that in Britain there are still many, whether a majority or minority, who see nothing wrong with corporal punishment and would certainly use it themselves. This is far from the child-centred view which in some countries has prevailed to the point where corporal punishment inflicted by parents is also illegal; though how far the principle is accepted in practice in these countries is hard to discover.

PARENTS' FREEDOM AND THE CURRICULUM

Religious education

Religious education is one area in which considerable attention has been given to the rights of parents. This is evident in the acceptance in Britain as in many other Western countries of the dual system of church and public schools and the greater or lesser amounts of public financing which most of these countries make available to support church schools of various denominations. Such a system enables parents to ensure that children receiving compulsory education at least have included in it the kind of religious teaching the parents want for them, and, theoretically, learn in a school with the desired kind of religious ethos. In some systems, however, parents have to make extra payments for this kind of education since public finance does not cover all costs: but in others, e.g. in Scotland, the Netherlands, and some Canadian states, this disadvantage does not apply.

Within the public school system there may be further safeguards for parents' rights in religious education. Thus the 1944 Education Act for England and Wales prescribed that schools should provide religious instruction and have school assemblies for acts of worship but it also allowed parents the freedom to withdraw their children from such teaching and observances. (Teachers' rights have been similarly safeguarded by acknowledgement that they are not obliged to give religious education.) What has been less satisfactory here is that parents have not always been aware of their rights or have been too apathetic to use them: hence the minority proposals in the Plowden Report that parents should be invited to 'opt in' – i.e. make a positive statement that they wanted their children to receive religious education – rather than passively accept that their children would receive it. Another problem has been, as we shall see later, that schools have often changed their interpretation of religious education without necessarily making parents aware of the change.

Parents and sex education

This is a new area of controversy since many schools until recently have not considered that they should provide sex education; and many have been afraid of an adverse parental reaction if they did so. But sex education has been more and more frequently introduced in schools and public opinion polls in England and Wales in 1986 suggested[6] that in fact well over 90 per cent of parents think it should be provided in schools, as do similar proportions of teachers and pupils. What still remains controversial is the content of such education, the ages at which it is given and especially the values with regard to sexual behaviour which it may or may not imply. For some parents, of course, these values are a matter of religious principles: for others, they are not. Teachers also, as we shall see in Chapter Seven, differ in their values and judgements here. Hence it remains uncertain who is to decide about the contents of sex education in the curriculum. In England it has been proposed that parents should have the right to withdraw their children from sex education, as they may withdraw them from religious education: but no general legislation has been passed. Individual withdrawals can indeed create practical difficulties, not least in ensuring no peer-group communication of the lessons which are thus missed – the peer-group has for long been an (unreliable) source of information on such matters. As an uneasy compromise, the decision in England has meanwhile been left to the governors of individual schools.

Other subjects of the curriculum

Individual parents have really little choice as to which other subjects their children are to be taught. Certainly they can advise their children when the school offers some options at the secondary stage, but if the school is not providing certain subjects, the only practicable step for the parent is to make such provision out of school. A parent, for example, who wanted his or her children to learn Latin or another foreign language not commonly offered in the system would be unlikely to affect the school's policy, especially as the counter-argument of unreasonable public expenditure could be used. Nowadays a parent whose child attends a single-sex school might complain that it is a case of sex discrimination if the child is not being taught subjects formerly regarded as suited to the other sex – girls not being taught metalwork, for instance, or boys receiving no tuition in domestic economy: but such cases are rare. Only if a fairly large group of parents demands an additional subject is the individual school curriculum likely to be affected. (Again we note the difference between countries where the curriculum is centrally determined and those where it is a matter for the local authority and even for the individual school.)

Similarly in cases where an individual parent objects to some part of a subject being taught – e.g., to the use of a certain book or theory – the parent is unlikely to effect change, unless supported by other parents or by a formal parents' association.

THE ALIENATION OF PARENTS

This survey of the limits set on parents' freedom to make decisions about their children's education shows how easily parents could come to the conclusion that the formal education of their children has been taken over and they themselves might as well cease to be concerned about what is going on. The gradual elimination of the need to pay fees, once universal compulsory education was established, probably contributed to this feeling of not being involved; though, as we have remarked, some parents continue to pay fees in order to obtain for their children a kind of education which they think the public system does not offer. But the general detachment of parents from schools was probably strengthened by the attitudes of teachers and local authorities. Not all teachers would necessarily have agreed with one traditional teacher's remark that, like the model Victorian child, 'the good parent is neither seen nor heard' but in many instances schools made it plain by formal notices and otherwise that parents should not come to interrupt the work of the school. Parents, too, might feel unwilling to enter the school if their own experiences of school had been unhappy or if they were over-awed by the greater learning and social status of some teachers. In such circumstances, when parental appearances were associated mainly with a crisis or vehement complaints, teachers' lack of enthusiasm for contact with parents is easy to understand. Yet it must be remembered that not all parents have felt this alienation: some schools (rural schools especially) have maintained good contacts.

THE RENEWAL OF PARENT PARTICIPATION IN EDUCATION

For many reasons parents are now being invited back into the activities of schools. Possibly this movement, evident since the 1970s in many countries, notably in France and Italy,[7] arises from growing awareness of the bad effects of parental apathy on the education of children as well as from democratic principles. Some researches showed, in the days when selection for secondary education was common practice, that the parents' frequency of contact with the primary school, and their concern for their children's progress, were positively related to the children's success in the selection examination: so parental interest was perceived as helpful. Better educated parents have themselves claimed greater attention to their points of view. Concern for democratic participation in the country's educational system, stimulated possibly by the mass media, has grown as has the understanding in schools that parents' contribution to education goes beyond ensuring that the children attend school in a clean and non-verminous state (requirements which early educational legislation rather emphasised).

What then are the ways in which parental cooperation with schools is now being encouraged? Which legislative provisions try to ensure that parents' opinions do affect what happens in individual schools and influence general decision-making about education? How reasonable and successful does this movement seem? Which principles justify it or render it suspect?

We find a great variety of ways in which schools in different parts of the world have contacts with pupils' parents, for example in the school and class councils of France and Italy as well as in the parents' councils at state and federal level in West Germany. Such contacts are officially prescribed in these and other systems: formal arrangements must be made for meetings of councils or committees at the various levels and for the election of parent members of such bodies. In some countries, for instance in the Soviet Union and East Germany, it is also regarded as the duty of the teacher to visit the pupils' homes: in other countries, or in certain areas of some countries, this would be seen as an invasion of privacy. But alongside formal provisions there are also arrangements by individual schools and parents which provide for a rather different kind of contact, sometimes on the initiative of the school, sometimes on parental initiative. (Visits by parents to teachers' homes to offer a bribe for better marks for their children come perhaps at one extreme of such contacts – they do happen in some systems, nevertheless.)

It is therefore useful to review some of the common ways in which parents may become involved with the schools or the educational system generally. In making such a review we have to try to assess the status accorded to parents in such contacts and the characteristics of parents which make their involvement valuable or less valuable. We have to be clear as to the benefits to be achieved. Enthusiasm for the involvement of parents can be undiscriminating: if they are asked to take part in pointless exchanges, no progress will be made – as we shall see, arrangements, powers and responsibilities have to be carefully considered if feelings of frustration and disillusionment are to be avoided, both among parents and among school authorities. Membership of a committee is not necessarily equivalent to exercising real influence on what happens in education. In addition, the role of the teaching staff of schools has to be kept in mind and the views of teachers, possibly also of pupils, attended to if this renewal of parental participation is going to become a genuine reform.

INFORMAL CONTACTS WITH SCHOOLS

In a variety of ways parents in different areas have become involved with the work of their children's school. They may, for example, serve as classroom assistants, especially in classes for young children, or they may provide clerical assistance. Some mothers work as 'dinner ladies' serving or possibly supervising school meals. Some parents help in school extra-curricular activities, giving talks or demonstrations to school societies; or they help with school sports or contribute to the careers guidance activities by telling of their own work or arranging visits to their place of employment. It is impossible to quantify such involvement since it is very much a matter for individual schools and it depends greatly on the circumstances of parents as well as their interests and skills.

More recently there have been increasing attempts to involve parents – most often, mothers – in helping their children to learn to read by listening to them reading (which, of course, many mothers have long been doing) and encouraging their reading. In schools where many children's home language is not English, mothers have also been brought into classrooms as helpers.

Rather more formal are the arrangements made by schools for 'Open Days' or 'Open Nights'. On such occasions parents are invited to visit the school to see exhibitions of work, or, possibly, on day visits, to watch classes going on 'normally': discussions with individual teachers may be included on these occasions. These events give the school an opportunity to explain and display its work, as well as allowing teachers and parents to become acquainted. Some enterprising schools have been known to organise open days when a strike has been affecting local industries, on the assumption that this would give fathers who normally would be out at work during the day a chance to get to know their children's school. With the increase in the numbers of mothers who are out at work, this assumption would now be rather 'sexist': but there probably has been a tendency in many places to expect the mother rather than the father to be involved with the children's education, since this has traditionally been regarded as a feminine interest. The strength of this tradition was recognised by one visitor-speaker to a parents' association meeting – 'How astonishing that 90 per cent of parents are women!' But social class also affects this situation.

Sports Days and Speech Days (the latter, as prize-giving functions, are becoming much less frequent in Britain) probably have a more limited appeal since they tend to focus on the performance of some pupils only, and therefore on the interests of a smaller number of parents. Some other meetings organised by schools are deliberately selective when parents of a certain year-group or year-groups are invited to talks and discussion about some matters – option choices, curriculum, examinations – specifically affecting these pupils.

Of course the traditional system of school report cards, to be signed by parents, should not be overlooked. Here also can be seen attempts to involve parents more closely by making the cards easier to understand (with no more use of ambiguous teacher's comments like 'trying'). Parents too may be asked to write their own comments about the evaluation of their child's progress. Some schools also use the system of daily or weekly report cards for individual children who have not been working or behaving well so that parents are made aware of the problem at the time it occurs and should know whether the problem is being eliminated, by their own intervention or by school action or both.

The system in some countries, West Germany for example, by which parents can 'sit in' on ordinary lessons in the school classroom does not seem widespread – we shall discuss later possible teacher reactions to it: but it is undoubtedly one way in which parents can become aware of what happens in school, even if it is likely again to be used only by a minority of parents. Also found in West Germany is the system by which teachers let parents know at which hours during the (secondary) school day they are available individually for consultation about pupils. Again, there are limits to the usefulness of such arrangements but this is one way of signifying to parents that communication is possible and even welcome.

FORMAL ORGANISATIONS

The most common forms of parental associations with schools are the parents' associations and the parent-teacher associations. These may vary greatly in purposes and in strength. Some, attached to individual schools, may be concerned with fund-raising for additional equipment and resources: some may be intended to be mainly social, bringing teachers and parents together in agreeable activities (though some teachers may react as did one disgruntled colleague who said that, after a hard day's work, he saw no earthly reason to go back in the evening to play bingo with a bunch of parents). Some meetings are intended to be mainly educative, giving parents a chance to learn about new developments in education, or to discuss common problems in bringing up children. Others may try to discuss and influence matters referring to the school's programme and work and may be joined in a federation of such associations having interests in the system of education generally.

We move here from arrangements made to enlist the interests of individual parents in the progress of their own children, and to allow parents to express their views about matters which affect their own children, to arrangements which enable parents as a group to express views about the work of the school in general or the performance of the educational system in general. This distinction is not always recognised but it is important since the authority to be given to parents' views in the different contexts is different. Parents have competence in bringing to attention circumstances which seem to be affecting their own children adversely: their competence to judge how education generally should be carried out and what its purposes should be is more questionable – they are not professionals in this area. Certainly, in a democratic society it is important to know the views of different groups concerning questions of public policy but different weight must be given to the opinions of different groups when specialist activities are involved. Parents talking about their own children and conditions in their children's schools merit considerable attention: parents giving opinions on the complex questions of educational policies and methods speak with much less knowledge and authority.

In parent-teacher associations, in England and the United States, there is usually concern with matters affecting the individual school and a general interest in curriculum and new developments in so far as they affect the school. Such associations may join in a federation concerned with wider issues but their main interests are usually specific. Where parents' associations join in federations, as in France, and express views on more general aspects of the educational system, the associations are likely to have a political affiliation or bias. They become public pressure groups which in some countries exercise considerable influence and engage in social action at a different level from the individual parent-teacher association.

In all formal organisations of parents, a fact frequently regretted is that some parents remain apathetic and do not participate. There is also a common complaint that in the larger organisations for parents, dominating roles are played by the middle-class, confident, articulate parents; so the views of the organisation may not be representative of the whole group of parents and some parents may be discouraged from participating. (This does not imply that working class parents are less interested than others in their children's education or that all middle-class parents are deeply interested: it is simply that for various reasons middle-class parents tend to take more active parts in school meetings – though of course much depends on the social background of the school.)

PARENTS AS MEMBERS OF COMMITTEES OR GOVERNING BODIES

This question of dominance by parents of a certain social class, education or personality, is relevant also to arrangements for including parent members on committees or other councils or boards which have responsibility for matters affecting an individual school or the education system generally. Often, these parent members are to be elected by the whole group of parents in a school (or in a federation). What is not clear is whether such parents are *delegates* of the other parents, with responsibilities for putting forward views agreed by the other parents and reporting back to them, or whether they are simply *representatives* who can freely express their own views and have no special responsibility for maintaining contact with those who have 'elected' them. Very often it is evident that the latter is the case. Moreover, when we look at such 'elections' there may be very little expression of public choice: in schools in some parts of Britain general apathy may mean that any parent willing to accept nomination will be 'elected' – thus we have, in a way, a self-selected group (which may include admirably public-spirited and knowledgeable people). In some cases it is a matter of the school head or the local education authority 'persuading' certain parents to accept office. The committees, councils or other bodies thus have a token inclusion of parental opinion but it cannot be said that they are necessarily in touch with the views of the whole parent body. (Again, much depends on the individual representatives' concept of their function and their willingness to think about and consult with the parents whom they 'represent'.) The same problems arise for teacher representatives on such bodies, and for pupil representatives or student representatives when they are included. Communication with their 'constituency' may sometimes be relatively easy to arrange: but it will not be arranged if the role of the representative is not clear. It can of course be assumed that any parents (or teachers, pupils or students) are likely to have much the same opinions as any others of their kind on educational matters: but even if this is so, the people not present at such discussions and hearing nothing about them are unlikely to feel their opinions have been expressed and noted.

A further problem for parent representatives is their ability to cope with the structures of discussion in the committees or councils to which they are elected or nominated. In many cases parents have reported that they found themselves unable to put their views because they were perplexed by a formal agenda or inhibited by the attitude of other members who apparently did not expect them to put critical or divergent views – or indeed to speak at all. It has now been recognised that parents generally need some training or preparation for coping effectively with formal meetings of the kind they encounter and in England, under the 1986 Act, local education authorities were obliged to provide training and information for school governors: some money has been made available for such preparation (some authorities were already providing it) but where provision is made, it has often, so far, been slight.[8] In France too the problems of the parent at committee meetings have been recognised (together with the sometimes unhelpful attitudes of teacher members towards parent representatives) and there some parents' association federations have also provided training.

PURPOSES OF PARENT REPRESENTATION

The contributions expected from parent representatives must depend on the functions and powers of the committee or council or board of governors. Here we can perhaps see advantages in some of the lower levels of school committee found in France and West Germany. In France, for instance, there are parent representatives (usually two) on the class council. This council, consisting of the teachers of a class or year group, other school authorities and parent and pupil representatives, considers matters relating to the work of that particular class or year group. Similarly, there is the school discipline council where problems of discipline are dealt with by teacher, parent, pupil representatives – obviously excluding members who would be personally involved in a given case. But even here there have been complaints that parent and pupil representatives feel themselves powerless, although the functions of the group seem straightforward and clearly defined.

In Scotland where parent representatives are important on the School Councils (with one Council per school or per group of schools), there have also been complaints that, although the Councils have been asked to consider various matters affecting the schools (including truancy), members have the impression that they are not doing anything of value or having a real effect on what happens in schools.

In England, the 1980 Education Act, implementing recommendations of the Taylor Report,[9] ensured the appointment of two parent governors to each maintained school's governing body. In practice such parent-governors are appointed in a variety of ways, some apparently more satisfactory than others. As we have noted, the need for training to cope with the business of meetings – as well, possibly, as with the reactions of other members – has been widely recognised: but the definition of the functions and powers of such governors remains vague, as does provision for communication between them and parents in general.

Official pronouncements suggest that in England central government hopes that the schools' boards of governors will raise the standards of education and ensure good teacher performance. But how they will do this is not explicitly stated. They have been given, for the present, responsibility for deciding on the sex education provision in their own school and they have also rather loosely defined powers in such matters as suspension or expulsion of pupils but the balance of power between governors and other authorities remains uncertain.

Many such uncertainties about what parent governors, and other group representatives, are supposed to do on school committees or educational councils arise from the amount of control of the educational system exercised by central or local government. Finances are clearly not a matter in which much flexibility is possible: teachers' pay and other major expenditures are government controlled; and not all local authorities are ready to allow individual schools some choice in deciding how the school's budget is to be spent. There are also official agencies to deal with truancy, delinquency and other problems. In such circumstances can an additional group of people, not professionally trained, exercise real authority? In countries where there is a centrally determined curriculum (and in Britain there are now moves towards this), individual school management decisions are further restricted – as they are also restricted by examination and qualification systems. Thus, many decisions affecting the individual school are largely made from outside: how can parent-governors or others exert genuine influence? Within the school, there is also the question of the authority of the head and staff to take decisions affecting the work of the school. For many teachers indeed the existence of the school's governing body remains nebulous (except in cases of dramatic controversy): many would point out that the teachers do the real work of education and these governing bodies are simply outsiders whose contribution is superfluous.

TEACHERS VERSUS PARENTS

It should not be implied that teachers and parents are likely to be adversaries in educational matters – far from it. But undoubtedly the proposals to bring parents to participate in the work of the schools cause uneasiness to many teachers. To avoid hostility or misunderstandings the circumstances of this participation and reasons for it should be thought about carefully.

Teachers would agree that individual parents should know about the progress of their own children: they should discuss that progress and make enquiries or complaints about it or even express enthusiasm and support for the school's work. Teachers indeed can benefit by such parental interest: if the parents know what is going on in school and what is expected of the learners, then they are better able to reinforce the school's work. Pupils also benefit by such understanding between school and home even if they lose the possibility, which some enjoy, of playing off one side against the other.

Teachers also appreciate the contributions of parent associations in raising funds for extra amenities and the informal help in school activities which, as we have seen, many parents give.

When it comes to decisions about teaching methods, teachers will consider that they are better able to decide than parents. Teachers have studied various methods and know their advantages or weaknesses. Teachers also have superior knowledge of how children in fact respond to different methods: and they know, as parents who are not teachers cannot know, the effects of the class situation on choice of method and on pupils' personality and behaviour. (Hence the doubts of some teachers as to how much parents are likely to understand if they observe, briefly, the classroom situation, the more so as, if their presence is a rare departure from normal conditions, parents may create a new situation and so get a false impression of the usual course of events.) Similarly, in matters of school discipline, teachers have greater knowledge of underlying principles and of practical aspects. These superiorities do not mean that teachers should proceed on their chosen way without explaining to parents the reasons for their actions or decisions but they do mean that the teachers' professional knowledge and competence should be recognised in any school discussions with parents. They do not stand on an equal footing in such respects (assuming that the teachers have indeed benefited by professional training).

When it comes to matters of morals the situation is more difficult to decide. We saw earlier that the Danish Advisory Council on Education stated that the school cannot remain neutral in some areas of controversy. The teachers in a school must therefore be clear which social values they try to inculcate, even if these values are not always those of the parents. In some cases, it may appear that parents are holding to prejudices which society in general would not accept. One example of current interest is belief in sex-stereotypes. Here teachers may try to encourage pupils not to be bound by such stereotypes and may give advice about the choice of subjects or careers which runs counter to the old prejudices, even if the parents still hold these prejudices. (Again, the school would of course try to explain this policy to parents; but it does not follow that parents will change their minds.) Another area of prejudice which schools may try to alter is that of racism and, again, some parents may not welcome such teaching. (It is also to be recognised that at present teachers themselves may not be in full agreement on such issues.) The school's justification in such cases, in addition to argument from principles, is likely to be that the views being presented are commonly accepted in society as a whole: but the school staff must be prepared, having thought about the purposes of their work, to put forward a reasoned, professional justification of what they are doing. In educational systems where the curriculum and its guiding principles are centrally defined the school could simply refer to government authority stating the accepted principles: but that, though perhaps simpler, is not necessarily the ideal response. This is a matter to be further discussed when we come to the school's function in educating for moral behaviour.

We may also note that one of the functions of the school is to educate parents. At various times in educational history it has been pointed out that parents are inadequately prepared to care for and guide their children, though at other times the teachings of their church have tried to make good this deficiency in some aspects. Some educators have tried to produce books for parents, telling them what children should learn and how they can be helped to learn – some of the greatest books on education in the past were written for such purposes, for instance, John Locke's *Thoughts Concerning Education*.[10] Modern writers are probably less ambitious, usually devoting themselves to some part of education – to early childhood, to cognitive development or to discipline. Dr Benjamin Spock's book on *Baby and Child Care*[11] is said to have decided how parents reared their children in a considerable number of countries. Such education for parenthood is best provided when the need is actually present: attempts to give it in advance in the school curriculum are likely to seem irrelevant for most pupils, and to be forgotten before the education can be put into practice (though of course schools' education of character and attitudes is generally relevant to good parenthood). Since not all parents are likely to read books or even magazine articles on how to educate children there is a need for provision by agencies naturally in touch with parents: ante-natal clinics, nursery schools and other organisations can provide advice on good parenting in the early years: schools can continue the process through discussions at parent-teacher meetings and through other contacts.

CHILDREN'S RIGHTS VERSUS PARENTS' RIGHTS

In many of the aspects of education discussed so far it has been assumed that parents' freedom is in the best interests of the children. But it is clear that, even apart from cases where parents fail to treat children well, there are points where exercise of the parents' freedom may mean a denial of the child's freedom. Compulsory education has tried to protect the child's right to education: but parents' choices still determine for many children how much education beyond the compulsory level they receive. An illustration of this is found in the British system of means-testing student grants and stating a notional 'parental contribution' to the maintenance of students. Not all parents give their children this parental contribution, sometimes possibly because of financial difficulties but sometimes through unwillingness to accept this responsibility – so their children suffer. At an earlier stage, the end of compulsory education, it appears that parents in the United Kingdom are now less likely than formerly to exert pressure on their children to leave school at this point: usually the decision does seem to be left to the young people concerned: yet some parents still encourage early leaving in cases where the best interests of the young person would be served by staying in full-time education. Parents too may exert pressure towards taking some kinds of employment – or seeking certain kinds of employment – rather than following the young person's own interests in learning. Here schools may try to protect young people's rights by discussion with parents and by advice to parents. Whether university teachers or local education author-ities can similarly intervene concerning parental contributions is doubtful. A complication in higher education arises in the very recognition by recent legislation that the young people 'come of age' at 18. This legal status, while a formal acknowledgement of the rights of the young, is not always compatible with continuing financial dependence on parents.

Other complications arising from recognition of young people's rights are evident in controversies concerning information about contraceptives and provision of contraceptives through educational institutions or otherwise. In some higher and further education institutions the provision of vending machines for contraceptives has been demanded by students not only for practical reasons but as, apparently, a symbolic recognition of their right to determine their own behaviour. Whether current concerns about AIDS will greatly affect parental attitudes in such matters remains to be seen. But another relevant conflict, less directly affecting educational institutions, between young people's rights and parents' rights is evident in the controversy concerning the confidentiality of medical consultations where advice may be given to girls concerning contraception or abortion. Limits set by the legal age of consent are obviously important here: but it also appears that some parents would wish to exercise considerable control over their children's freedom to determine their own actions with regard to intercourse or pregnancy. (One parental argument, not always consistently thought through, may of course be that the parents will probably have to provide for babies born as the result of too early or irresponsible adolescent parenthood.)

It is also to be noted that in **another** controversial area, that of religion, young people's rights to choose for themselves are recognised in some educational systems. In West Germany, for example, young people can choose to opt out of religious education after the age of 14. Presumably it can be argued that in adolescence young people reach the point of being able to judge for themselves in such matters (and whether this is formally recognised or not, it is commonplace that in adolescence there is often a breakaway by the individual from the family habits of religious observances). But in many school systems adolescent rights in this matter are not recognised.

In various other aspects of life too adolescents may opt to live differently from their parents, e.g. in matters of diet or health. They reject the way of life their parents wish them to follow. The question for schools is then whether to support the parents by reinforcing the customs and beliefs of the parent groups or to show pupils the acceptability of other ways and beliefs and encourage them to exercise their right to choose. Parents anxious to preserve their own culture and way of life may resent such school teaching. If the school finds that the parental ways are contrary to those held generally in the society in which the young people are going to live, then the school can claim to intervene on behalf of society. But it may also intervene because of the principle that human beings have the right to decide their way of life on rational grounds and are not bound to continue in the way set by the parent group. In that case there is an incompatibility between parental demands for the preservation of their way of life and the young person's right to make rational choices. The school, trying to educate rational, autonomous individuals, claims to support the rights of the young. The conflict may not always be acute: parents may decide that a well-balanced choice would indeed favour their way, and thus accept that the school is entitled to show other possibilities: and of course parents may also rely on the considerable emotional ties which their care and concern for the children have created over the years – their relationship with their children is likely, in most cases, to be much more decisive than the relationship between pupils and teachers. Yet in many cases a conflict between parents' rights and young people's rights is inevitable.

A further practical recognition of children's rights is to be noted. This is the legal provision in some countries for children to divorce themselves from their parents, i.e. to apply to be cared for by other people. Recently in Australia[12] a 15-year-old applied for such a separation: Sweden also has had such cases. There are obviously problems in assessing the reasonableness of such demands: parents may argue that the young person is simply objecting to proper discipline (there is of course other provision if the child is being physically ill-treated). It has to be judged whether it is in the interests of society as well as of the young person if the separation is approved and whether the alternative parents, as well as receiving the approval of the young person, will be socially responsible parents. (It is not clear whether a further 'divorce' after some time would be possible.) A curious variant on such divorcing could be the action of the young person in denouncing parents for illegal drug use (as has occurred in some cases in America). The young person presumably acts in the interests of society here – but simultaneously makes it probable that parents and child will be separated. Recent encouragement of children to report sexual abuse by parents, while protecting children's rights, may also have this corollary of subsequent separation or break-up of the family. Children reporting abuse may, in some cases, be initiating divorce from their parents.

CONCLUSIONS

Parents' rights in the education of their children have been considerably eroded by the interventions of society and such erosion has probably been beneficial to many children who would otherwise have been disadvantaged by parental apathy or ignorance. At the same time, there are dangers of increasing parental apathy by excessive take-overs of education.

Some parents are now reasserting their rights in various ways and there is a movement in many parts of the world to involve parents more closely with the work of the formal educational system. This involvement needs careful analysis if the best forms of contact between home and school are to be developed. In particular the distinction has to be made between parents' concerns with the education of their own children in individual schools and parental views on education in general. Contacts with schools should certainly be of a nature to involve all parents.

Where parental views on education in general are sought, there must be consideration of what the parents' qualifications to offer such judgements are – do they, for example, know what happens in other schools or other systems? Have they seriously studied the educational policies in question? The parental group in society is a large and heterogeneous group which scarcely seems likely to offer agreed and coherent views: individual parental groups may well speak most usefully on matters within their immediate experience. (It must of course be remembered, in talking about parents, that the majority of teachers are also parents.)

Limitations on parental freedom in education have been introduced by society for the good of the individual child and of society. At the same time it is evident that interventions by society may be ill-judged and benefit neither individual nor society. Professionals in education and administration can make mistakes. Familiarity with the characteristics of hundreds of children and young people may lead them to misunderstand, in some cases, what the potential and characteristics of the individual are. It is here that parents, knowing the individual and strongly concerned for that individual's well-being, are essential to point out such errors of judgement and ensure that professional actions are indeed in the interests of their child as well as in the interests of society.

Questions

1. Which forms of contact between parents and schools seem most likely to be helpful (a) to parents, (b) to the school?

2. For what reasons are parents likely not to be in contact with the school?

3. What seem to be the advantages and problems of having parent members of (a) school governing bodies, (b) school committees?

4. For what reasons are parents likely to withdraw their children from the school system (in countries where this is legally possible)? What advantages or disadvantages are likely for children being educated at home by their parents?

5. Why have parents' rights in religious education been specially protected?

6. What principles seem to enter into the debate about corporal punishment in schools?

7. Are children today sufficiently protected against parents' freedom to choose in education?

8. In what respects is conflict between parents' rights and teachers' rights likely to occur?

9. Should children be allowed to divorce themselves from their parents?

CHAPTER 5

The behaviourist approach

Behaviourism offers one of the most optimistic theories about education. It suggests that education can do anything and everything. An early behaviourist, J. B. Watson,[1] summed it up: 'Give me a dozen healthy infants, well-formed, and my own specified world to bring them up in and I'll guarantee to take any one at random and train him to become any type of specialist I might select – doctor, lawyer, artist, merchant-chief, and yes, even beggarman and thief, regardless of his talents, penchants, tendencies, abilities, vocations and race of his ancestors.' The power of education, on this prescription, is awe-inspiring. The educator decides what kind of person should result from education. The educator then uses the methods indicated by behaviourist theory and the desired results are obtained. There is the possibility of creating a whole new world: or, as some critics would put it, a 'brave new world'.

Of course when we look at it more closely we find that J. B. Watson, like others, hedged his bets. He demanded certain conditions: the infants were to be healthy (already a considerable limitation) and they were to be brought up in a 'specified' environment – and that is not as easy to achieve as it might sound. Modern behaviourists would be less comprehensive in their claims than Watson: but it is still important to know the psychological basis of this approach to education.

BEHAVIOURIST PSYCHOLOGY

Behaviourist psychology was in many ways a reaction against the introspective methods which dominated psychology before and during the nineteenth century. If we want to understand human beings, behaviourists argued, we should concentrate on their behaviour, on what they actually do, rather than interpret them according to our own experience or even according to their verbal statements. Observable behaviour seems to provide more reliable evidence than introspection: it is open to checking by other observers: it can be studied and analysed without any unprovable hypotheses about what may be going on 'in the mind'. This study of behaviour may avoid the usual human weakness of assuming that other people share our preferences and feelings. Whether verbal statements may count as behaviour is something that has proved controversial: on strict interpretations, in the early days, they would not be considered reliable but later approaches have used what people say, or their verbal responses to questions or situations, as evidence. Generally, concentration on observable actions has offered psychology a chance to be 'scientific', in the sense in which that word is used in methods and experiments of the physical sciences. Behaviours can be accurately observed, measured and analysed: different observers of the same behaviours should come in this way to the same conclusions.

Since behaviour was to be observed without assumptions about mental processes accompanying it, observations of the behaviour of animals acquired great importance. Highly influential was Pavlov's work on the conditioning of reflexes in animals. His experiments on training dogs to salivate in response to a sound rather than to the original stimulus of something to eat have become very widely, if vaguely, known. This discovery of the possibility of changing behaviour, even such basic behaviour as reflex actions, by controlled treatment led to an immense amount of research. Such research has included conditioning other kinds of behaviour (not simply reflexes), that is, causing certain behaviours to occur in response to a stimulus which was not originally connected with them. This research has also moved to 'operant' conditioning in which the subjects take action (e.g. animals press a certain lever to obtain food) rather than remain passive while the experimenter stimulates reflex responses. In such cases the action may originally occur by accident but it is then reinforced – that is, made more likely to happen again – because it is followed by satisfactory consequences: thus, the animal presses a lever and a food pellet is obtained: the animal presses again, another food pellet comes: so the lever-pressing behaviour is reinforced. Such reinforcement can be continuous – that is, happen every time the behaviour occurs – or intermittent, happening perhaps every third or fourth time the lever is pressed. Eventually, the reinforcement may be faded out, and no longer given. It can be reapplied if the behaviour is ceasing to occur: but in many cases, with humans as well as laboratory animals, the behaviour seems to become self-reinforcing and the need for additional reinforcement disappears. Alternatively, other reinforcements may become effective. Thus, in human situations, where children are 'reinforced' for certain behaviours by being given a token – coin or small stick which can later be used to obtain rewards like sweets, fruit or soft drinks – the stage may be reached where receiving the tokens is itself sufficient reinforcement. The choice and use of reinforcements or of aversive stimuli which eliminate some behaviours is a highly important part of behaviourist technique.

Behaviourism has also developed into various kinds of stimulus-response theories,[2] which have in common the study of the ways in which desired responses to a given stimulus can be produced and made habitual and the ways in which such connections are effectively made. An early influence was Thorndike's work with animals which tried to establish the Laws of Learning, that is, the conditions in which the right responses to chosen stimuli will be firmly fixed in the animal's behaviour. (Obviously, the kind of learning considered here is somewhat restricted.) Thorndike and other researchers in this area arrived at laws[3] concerning human and animal learning which, in retrospect, do not seem altogether astonishing: e.g. the law that the new association between stimulus and response is more likely if the two are presented close together in time; the law that an action is more likely to be repeated if it is followed by satisfactory consequences; the law that more frequent repetition leads to a stronger association. But the point was that some of these 'common-sense' associations had been established now by controlled observations and experiments; and sometimes the findings were not as might have been expected. These attempts to state succinct 'laws' also had effects in clarifying thought about learning.

CONDITIONING EMOTIONS

Experiments with animals had advantages in being relatively easy to control and in giving fairly rapid results concerning animal learning. Yet probably the rather unscientific experiment carried out by Watson and his associates to show how a young child could be conditioned to feel fear of something the child did not naturally fear aroused greater interest. Watson held that very few emotions are innate in humans and that they are evoked by a very small range of stimuli. A loud noise, he believed, does naturally evoke a fear response: so he arranged that when a small child, Albert, was about to respond normally and happily to a furry rabbit, a loud noise was made behind the child. After some repetitions of this situation Albert responded with fear and avoidance behaviour to the appearance of the rabbit. It was further demonstrated that this fear spread to other furry or fluffy things, though it is not certain exactly how far the experimenters claimed their results were generalised. At any rate, this was taken as an illustration of how human beings can acquire a large number of emotional responses to various objects and situations, simply by being conditioned by events in their environment.

An unkind extension of the theory holds that the child's attachment to the mother is simply a matter of being conditioned to associate her appearance with food and warmth rather than a manifestation of innate affectionate responses – it is indeed simply 'cupboard love'. (Much research has consequently been devoted to finding out whether young monkeys will respond to ingeniously varied mother substitutes – cushions, variously textured, or food supplies in various forms – as they do to the natural mother.)

It is at least reassuring to know that the same processes could be used to decondition such children as the hapless Albert. Repeated presentations of attractive food at the same time as the gradual reintroduction of the stimulus animal can remove the conditioned fear. But it is also interesting to know that a later psychologist,[4] C. W. Valentine, challenged Watson's thesis that fear of furry animals is not innate by carrying out an equally unscientific but fascinating experiment with one of his own children. He reported that when the noise stimulus was used in conjunction with a furry caterpillar the child did indeed show distress and avoidance of the animal: but when an attempt was made to condition responses to a pair of binoculars, it simply did not work – the child apparently did not learn to find this latter stimulus fearsome.

ASPECTS OF CONDITIONING

Whatever may be our response to such experiments, there has certainly been much work producing evidence about the possibilities of conditioning human behaviour by controlled use of chosen stimuli. Much of the work has also shown the complexity of the conditioning operation. It has demonstrated both the subtleties of human and other animal behaviour and the problems of controlling the environment to achieve the desired associations of stimulus and behaviour.

Notably, there has been research indicating the importance of personality variables. Introverts apparently can be conditioned more rapidly than extroverts. Some personalities can withstand many more uncertainties in discriminating which is the 'right' stimulus to respond to than can others. This indeed was evident in early Pavlovian work. If a range of stimuli was presented and the 'right' stimulus was very similar to those which were not to be responded to, some subjects could tolerate this uncertainty until the stimuli were almost indistinguishable: others had what could be described as a nervous breakdown as the problem of discriminating became more difficult. The uncertainty as to whether to respond or not apparently produced considerable distress. Explanations for such personality differences have been offered in psychological theories based on differences in the central nervous system: different individuals respond weakly or strongly, build up inhibitions against further responses quickly or slowly, and so on, according to the physiological properties of their central nervous system.

It has also become clear that it may be difficult to direct the subject's attention to the stimulus that interests the experimenter. Again, in laboratory situations, it has been found that the animals may begin to respond simply to the arrival of the laboratory assistants before the experimenter can get round to introducing the important stimulus – important, that is, from the experimenter's point of view.

Also unexpectedly, it has not always been possible to know which response was being evoked in experimental animals: instead of an interest in food, some have shown behaviour which would seem to indicate an interest in exploring – or simple curiosity. (Going to a fanciful extreme has produced alternative interpretations that the animals are interested in conditioning the experimenters.)

On the more positive side, however, it has also been discovered how conditioning can irradiate, so that a response becomes associated not simply with a particular stimulus but with other stimuli which are somehow related to it. Thus a conditioned reaction to the word 'hospital' can occur in response to such words as doctor, ward, operation. On a non-scientific level, many people are aware of the way in which dislike of, say, a certain subject in school can spread to dislike of school in general or teachers in general: or, more happily, how a certain song can arouse feelings of pleasure because of the romantic circumstances in which it was first heard. Also more positively, it has become evident that conditioning can be used to get rid of fears or other undesirable reactions: for example, some phobias can apparently be eliminated by a careful process of presenting milder forms of whatever stimulates the phobia, in comfortable surroundings, with relaxation and agreeable stimuli, so that gradually new associations with the stimulus are made and the fear responses are eliminated.

Yet it is not always clear whether behaviour acquired through conditioning will spread to situations other than the original situation: thus, for example, some autistic children may be taught to use language in the classroom situation but may not use what they have learned in the playground: or children who have learned to keep their possessions tidy in the residential school may not do the same at home. The conditioned response may be too narrowly connected with some specific situation.

Nevertheless, a great deal of research has shown the possibilities of affecting human behaviour by conditioning, that is, by associating desired responses with certain stimuli or situations and ensuring the future re-occurrence of the desired response by giving appropriate reinforcements or rewards. (On the negative side research has also shown the possibility of eliminating undesired responses by aversive stimuli – that is, by associating them with stimuli unpleasant to the receiver.)

SOCIAL ENGINEERING

This possibility of controlling and shaping human behaviour has widened out into considerations important for educators – or politicians. Putting it simply, if the environment can be controlled, so apparently can the behaviour of human beings in that environment. B. F. Skinner[5] especially has expressed the view that we can now arrive at a science of human behaviour which could be used to establish the ideal society. If human beings could be brought up in a suitable environment then, he asserts, bad behaviour would not happen because it would simply not occur to people to behave in undesirable ways. He suggests, for example, that 'we shall not solve the problems of alcoholism and juvenile delinquency by increasing a sense of responsibility. It is the environment which is 'responsible' for the objectionable behaviour, and it is the environment, not some attribute of the individual which must be changed.' Skinner rejects the view that this might be an attack on the freedom of the individual. The attempt to be free is, on his interpretation, the attempt to avoid 'aversive' aspects of the environment. When people apparently act 'freely' they are simply responding to earlier conditioning which has made them behave in certain ways. On this somewhat bleak interpretation, the human self is 'a repertoire of behaviours appropriate to a given set of contingencies'.

What is not explicit in this philosophy is the kind of culture which would be created if the environment and human behaviour could indeed be controlled as Skinner would hope. The question must arise: who would be the controllers? On what principles would they decide what was undesirable behaviour? Presumably, their choices would depend on their own earlier conditioning (as do the choices of those having authority in society as it exists at present). Skinner appears optimistic about the social control which would be exercised and suggests that the culture would go 'beyond the immediate interests of controller and counter-controller' towards 'the survival of the culture and of mankind'. In this respect he would apparently judge such qualities as being cooperative and supportive to be the kind of responses to develop: willingness to 'work for the good of their culture' would be worth having. Yet although one cannot take the fictional creations of such states as those shown in Aldous Huxley's *Brave New World* or Orwell's *1984* as necessarily showing the inevitable results of social engineering, they do draw attention to some possible outcomes if the human environment could be systematically and completely controlled by what would seem to us, given our own peculiar conditioning, to be the wrong kind of controllers. It is possibly fortunate that the complete control necessary for such conditioning of human behaviour is at present impossible to achieve. But it can be achieved to some extent, in some environments, on a smaller scale.

We should perhaps note here Skinner's approval of Rousseau's plan to control the environment in which his ideal pupil was to be educated. Yet Skinner did not accept other child-centred views: he found that leaving the child to learn 'out of interest' and natural curiosity merely produces someone who is lazy and prepared to argue that since knowledge is constantly changing there is no point in trying to acquire it. On the other hand, a later writer has suggested[6] that Rousseau was a better behaviourist than Skinner since Rousseau apparently tried not only to control Emile's behaviour but also the way in which Emile thought and the ideas which he would have.

Curiously enough, in countries which adopt the theory of collective education, behaviourist techniques do not seem to be much used in formal teaching, though possibly they may be traced in other forms of learning, especially in social behaviour. But many societies have recognised the importance of controlling the physical environment so far as possible, e.g. by regulations about buildings, public monuments, style of dress. Plato's scheme for the ideal state proposed harmony and beauty in the material environment, to be reflected in the harmonious development of the character of the citizens. On a smaller scale, Goethe suggested that the colouring of the walls of rooms affects the mood of the people in them: a cool blue-green seemed to him appropriate for a study and a golden yellow for a room where guests were to be entertained. Rather similarly the Rudolf Steiner schools emphasise the shape of rooms, colours of walls, coloured glass windows, as formative influences on the minds of the young. (Looking at the physical environment offered in some school classrooms today one can only hope that the conditioning offered by the content of lessons is much stronger than the conditioning offered by badly maintained, unlovely surroundings.)

BEHAVIOURIST TECHNIQUES IN TEACHING

If major social engineering is at present rather beyond the powers of the science of human behaviour, it is still worth considering what effects behaviourist principles have on how people teach or on how people might teach. Current research on what happens in classrooms frequently uses the technique of simply observing what people do and counting the numbers of times that a certain behaviour occurs. For example, the Flanders Scale which measures classroom interaction notes how often and for how long the teacher speaks and how often pupils speak – though it is probably significant that investigators usually find the need to supplement this by considering what kind of comment is made by teacher or pupils and what is the quality of any silence that may occur. Nevertheless, even such simple enumeration of behaviours has had a great effect on perceptions of what happens in classrooms, notably, the large proportion of time taken by teacher talk or the relatively lesser amount of talk from girls as compared to boys.

In the classroom the teacher is certainly a dominant feature of the environment. It has therefore seemed important to discover what kind of reinforcement of learning the teacher offers. Observers have counted the number of times the teacher makes an approving comment, smiles or otherwise gives positive reinforcement to the pupils' behaviours: they have also counted the numbers of times the teacher provides an aversive stimulus by disapproving comment, frowning or other behaviours. While the proportions of positive or negative behaviours differ from one teacher to another, the proportion of negative behaviours is apparently more often greater than the proportion of positive reinforcements. Teachers can of course offer valid reasons for such a situation: they might also argue that the major positive reinforcement is in doing the work well, not in the teacher's behaviour. Yet frequent negative reactions are possibly not the best way of encouraging learning and of conditioning pupils to have positive attitudes towards continuing school work.

In some researches teachers and therapists have been made aware of the balance between their positive and negative reactions and have consciously set about changing the proportion of positive reinforcement they give: good results, as shown in pupil responses, are reported to follow. Yet changing one's habitual behaviour can be difficult: automatic repetition of words of commendation may not carry conviction to the pupils and so it may fail to reinforce. (Analysis of this kind is of course relevant to parents in dealing with their children, as it is relevant to any kind of interaction between human beings where one may wish to change the behaviour of the other.)

Such analyses have also indicated the importance of consistency of response. If a behaviour does not meet always with positive reinforcement and is seldom reinforced, it may not be acquired or may soon fade out. Thus a child who has made a

special effort to do something well may need immediate reinforcement and may not make the effort again if it is lacking; for
difficult tasks, reinforcement may have to be continuous until the
behaviour is well established. Similarly, where the intention of
the teacher is to eliminate some forms of behaviour, aversive
responses have to be consistent and continuous – if indeed aversive responses are being used. (Some advocates of behaviourist
techniques propose rather to eliminate the undesired behaviour
by reinforcing alternative and acceptable behaviour.) Problems
also arise when the teacher is being resolutely consistent in
responding to certain behaviours but other important people in
the child's environment are being inconsistent or even reinforcing
the behaviour which the teacher is trying to eliminate.

The peer-group may well be one such reinforcer of behaviours.
If the teacher, for example, is trying to reduce the amount of
calling-out of irrelevant and irreverent comments by one pupil
the teacher may have decided not to reinforce such behaviour by
giving it attention. But the pupil in question may be finding
plenty of reinforcement in the attention given by the rest of the
class. Or, in other kinds of behaviour, the peer-group may give
reinforcement outside the classroom when the teacher is not part
of the environment. In such cases, it may be necessary to arrive
at group contracts with the class: or to recognise that the
teacher's power to reinforce or eliminate behaviour is largely
limited to the school situation.

If, for example, the teacher is concerned about the problem
of young people smoking, drinking alcohol or glue-sniffing,
verbal reinforcement for avoidance of these activities can be
given in school or rewards devised for the number of days on
which they are not indulged in. But the activities may be self-
reinforcing: at the time, they seem to be associated with pleasurable consequences: and they may also be reinforced by the
approval of companions. While the longer-term consequences are
indeed deterrent, there is too great a distance between the action
and the sequel to have an effect on present behaviour – putting
it differently, the discipline of natural consequences does not
operate because the consequences are not immediate or perceptible. Hence, in coping with such problems we need to devise
some control of the out-of-school environment (parents naturally
would need to be involved here) and to find some way of objectively monitoring the young person's behaviour and immediately
and consistently rewarding the 'right' responses.

Behaviourist analyses also criticise another aspect of school
practices, the gap which frequently occurs between pupils' behaviour and any intended reinforcement or deterrent response. If
work is left waiting for teacher comment for some time, the
connection between the carrying out of the work and positive

reinforcement by praise may not be made; so, too, bad work may not be related to the teacher's eventual criticisms or fury. (In higher education similar complaints have been made about the length of time taken by some tutors to mark essays.) Similarly, when certain behaviours are to be eliminated, traditional school punishments like giving lines or detention often leave a relatively large space of time between the bad behaviour and its consequences: hence the ineffectiveness of such punishments in altering behaviour. It could of course be claimed that in these cases the announcement of the punishment serves as a token and this may itself become a negative reinforcer rather than the actual punishment later: sometimes in schools this does seem to be what happens: or the announcement of the punishment is seen as a comprehensible statement of the teacher's disapproval and so serves as deterrent.

In this connection, some teachers have argued that corporal punishment had precisely the merit that it could follow immediately on the behaviour which was to be eliminated. This, however, does not counter the argument that in some such conditions peer-group reaction nullifies the effect of the punishment. There is the further alternative objection that the unpleasantness of corporal punishment may not attach simply to the behaviour which led to it but extend to the subject and the school.

Other behaviourist techniques have been developed for use when the behaviour of a group rather than of an individual is to be modified. One such technique is to define precisely the kind of behaviour which is wanted, e.g. quiet attention to the work in hand, and then make a contract with the class that if, when a check is carried out, the behaviour is being shown by the class, there will be a reward of, say, one point. If the class gains an agreed number of points a special reward will be given, for example, free time to talk quietly together during the last period of the day or week, or access to some other enjoyable activity. The checks on behaviour are carried out systematically at regular intervals, according to classroom conditions. This system is claimed to have produced noticeable results in the amount of time pupils do spend working quietly. What is less clear is the extent to which it will generalise to other school work or persist if the rewards are made intermittent or gradually phased out. Again, much depends on whether the activity of working quietly becomes self-reinforcing.

In such techniques, the choice of the reinforcement for the desired behaviour is a matter of some delicacy. It could be argued that to give the reward of not working during part of the school day is an odd way to build up a positive reaction to school work. Unkind critics would describe such action also as a resort to bribery. But finding good reinforcements is not easy. In trying to reinforce desired behaviours with maladjusted or handicapped children it has been customary to use pieces of chocolate or small sweets, which have the advantage of being easy to store and easily manageable. More recent concerns about the right diet for children (and adults) have made such choices seem contrary to the best interests of the child, though pieces of fruit may prove acceptable substitutes (if the child takes to them). Yet this problem of suitable rewards or reinforcers is an old argument since Rousseau disagreed with Locke as to suitable prizes or inducements for children: Rousseau thought it appropriate to appeal to the child's liking for sweet things but Locke had argued that we should not encourage the child to find satisfaction simply in pleasant physical sensations: we should rather encourage the child towards right behaviour by giving commendations – these would be ample reward for a child with self-esteem. What does seem crucial is whether the rewards in fact appeal to those who receive them and whether they do establish the behaviour on a long-term basis. (The system of giving or deducting 'house points' in some schools works when pupils regard the reputation of the 'house' they belong to as important: it fails when they have no interest in the 'house'.) Meanwhile it is interesting to reflect that the old-fashioned primary teacher with a jar of sweets and a cane on her desk was employing positive and negative reinforcements to determine her pupils' behaviour.

The contract system has also been employed with individual children who have shown disturbed behaviour. Here the essence of the technique is to make it clear to the child exactly what behaviour is to be engaged in and to set out a timetable (for a manageable period of time) during which engaging in that behaviour will receive stated rewards: or the behaviour which is not to be indulged in is similarly stated clearly and rewards are programmed for stated periods of time which are free from that behaviour. Again, this method has been claimed as giving good results, especially in a residential setting where all concerned know what the contract is. Similarly, the use of token awards to reinforce desired behaviours has been found helpful both in individual cases of disturbed children and in group situations.

THE TEACHER'S ROLE IN USING BEHAVIOURIST TECHNIQUES

From the foregoing discussion it will have emerged that the teacher is expected to define clearly exactly what behaviour is desired or undesirable and to specify the situations in which such behaviours are likely to occur.

It is also clear that the teacher is to remain dispassionate in using these techniques. Certainly the teacher may express attitudes by not responding to some behaviours, by 'turning a deaf ear' or 'not seeing' some attempts to claim undue or inappropriate attention. The teacher may also express approval, verbally or by eye contact or by smiling. But the teacher does not become emotionally involved with the situation since the way to deal with it is not by the expression of the teacher's personal reactions but by following the pre-determined course of action in reinforcing or not reinforcing certain behaviours. (Similarly the parent, trying to teach the child some behaviours by these techniques, should avoid emotional reactions and simply follow the planned programme.) This confident perseverance in using the technique does require considerable thought and self-control, especially in the unforeseen occurrences which often characterise dealing with the young.

BEHAVIOURISM AND PLANNING SCHOOL WORK

These techniques of detailed analysis of behaviour have also been recommended in deciding what the syllabus is to be in school subjects. They have produced the 'behavioural objectives' approach to curriculum planning. Instead of having a vague general statement of topics to be 'covered' in a series of lessons, teachers have to think precisely what changes should be apparent in learners' behaviour after the course has been taught. For example, it might be that 'pupils will use the future tense of the verb *aller* correctly in conversation' or 'pupils will make accurate measurements using a thermometer'. The matter to be taught is then divided into units corresponding to the changes in behaviour it is intended to make. In this way it is clear whether provision has been made to teach exactly what is intended: and it is easy, at the end of the course, to assess whether in fact the learners' behaviour has been changed as was intended.

Objections to such behavioural objectives have been frequent. It has been pointed out, for example, that while work is going on new aspects may appear or pupils may ask unforeseen questions and it would be undesirable to ignore these simply because they were not included in the behavioural objectives. More importantly it has been argued that not all outcomes of a course of teaching can be expressed in immediate behaviour. There may be little change in observable behaviour if, for example, appreciation of a poem has been greatly increased – one cannot really expect all the learners forthwith to buy copies of the work of that poet or begin writing similar poems themselves: yet this kind of outcome may be strongly intended by the teacher. Nevertheless, it is probably true that in many cases teaching becomes more purposeful if the objectives in terms of subsequent behaviours have been carefully thought out and it may in fact be possible to specify a wider range of objectives than initially seems probable to teachers thinking of using this method. It is always useful to ask ourselves what exactly we hope to achieve by our teaching – and sometimes to realise in answering this question whether or not there is a real prospect of achieving the intended results.

This approach has certainly influenced a number of other current techniques in teaching. There is, for example, the technique of precision teaching which involves the clear definition of what is to be learned and sets a timetable to control rates of progress. 'Graded objectives' for various subjects also follow the technique of trying to specify exactly what a learner should know or be able to do at a given stage. The award of certificates at the end of a module of learning instead of after a much longer period of study is another instance of giving reinforcement immediately after the behaviour has taken place.

If precise objectives for teaching are set in such ways, it may be claimed that the teacher's efficiency is shown by the extent to which the set objectives are achieved. Some teacher appraisal schemes propose this method of assessment. Teacher appraisal in this way could be regarded as unbiased and straightforward. It is therefore important for teachers to consider how effectively or reasonably objectives can be defined for the work they are doing and whether the attainment of their objectives can be assessed by measuring pupil performance. (Some interpretations of such appraisal would almost seem to be returning to the nineteenth-century regulations of 'payment by results' – and these scarcely offered a successful or satisfactory method of improving teaching. What was not realised by the authorities at that time was the difference between obtaining the stated behaviour – for example, bringing children to 'read' a page of print mechanically, a process rather aptly described by some critics as training them to 'bark at print' – and teaching so that the learners would understand and be able to use what had been taught. (The resourcefulness of teachers in securing surface compliance with set standards was then, as later, regrettably underestimated.) Obviously much must depend on who defines the behavioural objectives, how comprehensive they are and how well they are suited to the capacities of the learners.

PROGRAMMED LEARNING

Possibly one of the best known techniques related to the behaviourist approach is that of programmed learning. In its early development this method presented the learner with short, easily mastered units: successful response to questions on these units was rewarded with access to the next stage, possibly also with some words of congratulation. (Whether such formal statements of approval really served to reinforce the learning is doubtful: but the principle of reinforcement was being observed.) The method thus elicited the desired response – choice of the correct answer – and reinforced that response. The units were made so clear and simple that the probability of error was low: thus a continuous reinforcement and, presumably, development of positive associations with the learning process seemed likely.

Moving away somewhat from what could be regarded as pure behaviourist techniques, though still retaining some aspects, other developers of programmed learning have favoured a 'branching' technique which gives rather longer units and alternative sequences according to the learner's choice of answer and apparent need for fuller explanation, or revision of a point dealt with earlier, or rapid progress to a further stage.

Programmed learning has often been associated with teaching machines which present the material to be learned in various formats and make provision, usually, for the learner's active choice of answers (sometimes carefully trying to eliminate possibilities of cheating): but programmed learning books have also been produced. Rather similar approaches have been made in some developments of computer-assisted learning though more recent work in this area has emphasised rather the ways in which such learning can encourage the learner to be creative and develop new uses for the resources available.

In such applications of behaviourist techniques, it has often been emphasised that they have the advantage of freeing learners from personal comment and criticism by the teacher, thus providing a less emotional environment for learning: this is especially valued when criticism or comment have tended to arouse unpleasant feelings. Learning can proceed without negative associations. The enjoyment of using a teaching machine or computer is sometimes regarded as in itself a positive reinforcement of the learning process. But learners react differently to the use of such devices as teaching machines or microcomputers. Much depends on their earlier associations with these resources and how the resources are made available. It makes a difference if, for example, there are enough machines to allow easy individual access without competition or embarrassing publicity for any mistakes. Of course much also depends on whether the introduction to using the programme is well planned and develops learners' confidence in this situation.

Even so, carefully planned learning by such techniques may have its limitations. Research on learning of this kind and other learning without teacher intervention has shown that satisfaction in getting the right answer and in working with a programme or book are not always sufficient to ensure good progress. In various cases learners have shown the need for human interest: for example, 'distance learning' courses like those of the Open University have discovered that students are much helped by some personal contact with a tutor, even by telephone: brief attendance at residential summer schools gives not only additional cognitive learning but can greatly reinforce confidence and enthusiasm in learning. Students who have to learn by impersonal means alone often abandon their courses. Similarly when attempts have been made to teach students in higher education by letting them watch video-recordings it has been found that the presence of a tutor during learning sessions helps considerably. Interest on the part of another human being thus seems to be a most important reinforcer and sometimes is an essential reinforcer. (This can be a comforting thought for teachers who at times fear that their work may be taken over by machines.)

LANGUAGE LEARNING AND BEHAVIOURISM

Some early forms of behaviourist theory attempted to explain the acquisition of language in early childhood as an example of shaping the baby's behaviour by repeating, thus reinforcing, sounds which resembled words and so bringing the baby to utter correctly an increasing number of words. Learning that saying certain words was rewarded with changes in the environment led to reinforcement of a useful vocabulary. Gradually, the approval and comprehension shown as the child copied the speech of others would reinforce and increase the use of language. There have been considerable modifications of this explanation and great controversies between supporters of the behaviourist position and those accepting rather the theory of Noam Chomsky which assumes an innate capacity to acquire language and to understand linguistic structures. Other theories about language learning have challenged both the behaviourist and the Chomsky explanations. Certainly the capacity of young children to 'invent' word forms which they cannot have heard seems to contradict the elementary behaviourist theory: when the child says 'I goed' instead of 'I went' we do seem to have an indication that the child has not learned this from the environment but has become aware of a pattern in word formation and has applied it in a creative way. Yet it is also evident that some aspects of a young child's language use are distinctively shaped by the environment.

Behaviourist theory has however proved useful in developing

the use of words by autistic and other children who do not develop language in the usual way. The technique of shaping random sounds into useful sounds by rewarding and reinforcing their closer approximation to real words has proved effective: systematic presentations of a stimulus which the child comes to associate with a word, and rewards when the child utters the word appropriately, have increased the vocabulary of such children. There have sometimes been difficulties, as we noted earlier, in bringing the children to use such words outside the situation in which they have been learned but it is possible that extensions and modifications of the method will develop the desired generalisation.

In a rather different context, that of learning a foreign language, behaviourist techniques have also been used. They were for a time particularly popular in the structuring of drill exercises for use in language laboratories. Here one small grammatical point was presented at one time: a large number of examples of the use of the structure or phrase was offered for repetition by the learner, followed by very simple questions whose correct answer demanded use of the phrase or structure. In such learning there was little probability of wrong answers, though fluency in responding did require considerable attention and practice. The learner was reinforced by hearing the correct answer repeated by the voice on the tape (or the voice of the tutor); the frequent repetitions were designed to elicit an automatic response to a stimulus phrase. This technique was thought to lead to a much more satisfactory use of the language than the halting and inaccurate 'translations' which so many learners taught by traditional methods produce when they try to use the foreign language. The popularity of such drills has dwindled as it has been recognised that the automatic repetition could be highly unrewarding and that young and less able learners rapidly became bored and ceased to make the necessary efforts. It has also been recognised that the method introduces highly artificial contexts and that it does not allow learners to use the language for their own purposes, to communicate something to other people. Yet for adult learners, or those who are generally already highly motivated, this method can have some advantages in avoiding embarrassing public situations and in giving the opportunity to acquire correct and 'spontaneous' responses to fairly common uses of the language.

In using behaviourist techniques we keep meeting the interesting question of whether it is really best to learn without making any mistakes or whether the process of making mistakes and finding out why they are mistakes can be valuable. It may of course depend on the nature of what is being learned. For the behaviourist, certainly, learning should be as far as possible error-free. It should be presented in manageable units and the correct response should be clearly indicated and reinforced. Making mistakes, it is suggested, sometimes means that the wrong responses are built into the learner's behaviour and take much time and effort to eradicate.

WIDER IMPLICATIONS

These most recent examples have been concerned with the use of behaviourism within schools and other educational institutions. But it has been suggested that some behaviourist techniques are evident in the wider society, particularly in the influence exerted by the media and by commercial advertisements. Here it is argued that by repeated presentation of a stimulus and its association with some pleasurable experience, the reader or viewer learns to respond positively to that stimulus. For example, a certain make of car may be presented in association with people who are attractive to look at, healthy, probably rich or with at least a sufficiency of cash. It is thus 'learned' that buying that car is connected with these same attributes: at least the sight of the car in future will evoke positive feelings in a prospective purchaser. (There may of course be other more objective arguments advanced in favour of the car: but few advertisements concentrate on these alone.) Similarly, it is argued, many other associations are formed and responses which apparently are rewarded in media presentations may be learned and used.

A further possible effect of the media is suggested by some critics: there could be a process of deconditioning of responses of sympathy and concern. By repeatedly offering the stimulus of sights of human suffering when the observer is in relaxed and comfortable surroundings (watching television, for instance), and can make no active response, we may gradually eliminate the response of sympathising or helping.

Against these accusations of conditioning or deconditioning it can be argued that forming associations on this level, when the individual is not personally involved, is not an effective mechanism: it does not necessarily affect real behaviour. There is also the strong probability that factors in the real environment will rapidly decondition any unrealistic responses. This is something to be further considered when we discuss the education of emotions, but it does raise the question, to which behaviourism so far has no definite answers, of what thought processes occur when stimuli are presented and how the individual's possible awareness of the situation may affect the forming of associations.

EVALUATIONS OF BEHAVIOURISM

As we have seen, behaviourism offers considerable practical guidance to teachers, both in planning their work and in helping learners to make progress easily. Guidance is also offered as to the ways in which social behaviour may be shaped and determined. The teacher's role is shown to be one of scientific and controlled use of well-thought-out techniques.

The emphasis on methodical analysis of what is to be taught does seem to be of considerable value, even if not all educators would agree that such analysis must produce statements of objectives in the form of observable modifications of behaviour.

Behaviourist theories have also had the merit of producing a great deal of research on teaching situations. Results of these researches have had advantages not only in showing that some techniques do seem to achieve the intended effects but also in making people more aware of their own behaviour and the behaviour of pupils in the classroom situation. Behaviourists do try to test their theories by controlled observations.

Possibly one of the main negative responses to behaviourism is an uneasy feeling that it 'manipulates' other people. It tends to be associated with 'brain-washing' techniques, which can indeed be a form of application of behaviourist principles. Yet the techniques which have been proposed for educators' use do not seem to attempt to make people do things without realising what is going on. In stating behavioural objectives for a course of study, the educator is making it perfectly (or nearly perfectly) clear what the intended outcome is. In arriving at contracts with individuals or groups the educator is making explicit what behaviour is being proposed and will be rewarded. It is obvious when reinforcements are being given. Thus there is, in the use of behaviourism in education, little suggestion of subliminal conditioning or the application of reinforcements or aversive stimuli which the subject does not consciously perceive. Possibly some objects in the background of the learning situation – symbols, pictures, badges worn by teachers, even, as we have suggested, the decor of the surroundings – could be having conditioning effects but their influence seems likely to be comparatively minor. Conditioning in the wider society may take place without the individual's awareness of it, but in the learning situation the individual does know which behaviours are being reinforced or produced and this is so even when it is social rather than cognitive behaviour that is in question.

It can of course be argued that while the explicit curriculum of the school makes learners aware of what is intended, there is also a hidden curriculum which conditions them to make certain responses and to form certain expectations. Yet the hidden curriculum of schools does not seem an example of intentional application of behaviourist theories (unless we accept a conspiracy theory that somewhere some group or individual has defined objectives of giving some pupils repeated experience of failure, conditioning girls not to intervene in public discussions, etc., and planned school work accordingly). The hidden curriculum of schools would seem to be much more the effect of people acting according to their own earlier conditioning in an unreflective manner. Study of behaviours in school might indeed go far towards indicating needs for change in the hidden curriculum: some classroom observation studies have already had some such effects.

The unease about 'manipulating' other individuals seems indeed to arise from concern about hidden attempts to influence others. For it can otherwise be pointed out that the decision to teach is a decision to modify the behaviour or knowledge of other people. It would be pointless to take the view that such intervention is acceptable so long as it is not very efficient – that is, so long as the educator does not think precisely how to achieve the intended outcomes and does not think out the best ways of modifying behaviour. What seems important is rather the consent of the individual who is to be educated and the individual's awareness of the intended outcome.

It is probably in questions of individual awareness and individual consent that other doubts may be raised about behaviourist theory. For some people it is repugnant to think that our present behaviour depends entirely on earlier experiences reinforcing some actions and deterring us from others. Some, for instance, would claim for human beings the quality of 'free will', the capacity to determine actions by a conscious choice of principles. Others would affirm the naturalist or child-centred view that, innately, human beings have impulses to behave well and creatively. Religious teachings of different kinds present alternative views of human nature and the freedom of the individual to make choices.

There does indeed seem to be an area of uncertainty in behaviourist theory until recent times as to how much cognitive perception of our behaviour we have. It is unclear whether the forming of associations between certain stimuli and responses is accompanied by conscious interpretation of the situation and the formation of 'rules' for future behaviour. Speculation about such 'mental' or cognitive processes would have been anathema to earlier behaviourists concerned with what can be objectively established but some recent work has tried to bring together cognitive psychology and behaviourist psychology. There has been interest in trying to assess which kind of reference back to antecedent experiences is made and whether, as a result of conditioning experiences, human beings form strategies of response to future stimuli; whether indeed they produce 'meta-cognitive' strategies in which they are aware of their thought processes and responses to events, and decide their actions in accordance with plans based on earlier experience and its analysis. In providing therapy, various attempts have therefore been made to make explicit the relevant attitudes and beliefs of the individual who is to be helped instead of simply rewarding the desired behaviour. The individual may be encouraged to recognise, for instance, a situation arousing fear and to recall the strategies which have been effective in coping with it or to devise new strategies; and so come to produce the desired behaviour. This cognitive behaviour modification technique has given some promising results and may produce useful future modifications of theory.

At present it may be argued that behaviourism does not offer sufficient insight into the whole of human activities, especially into those not evident in observable behaviour. It can also be argued that it offers no clear ultimate aims for education: rather it seems to offer methods of achieving aims otherwise decided. Yet it does undoubtedly provide considerable insights into much of our behaviour in everyday circumstances. We do realise how past experiences have conditioned us to react positively or nega-tively to certain people and certain situations. (Perhaps a good example of this was Swift's doubtless well-meant birthday compliment to a friend, saying that she should not worry about age reducing her beauty for, just as we learn to associate good companionship and happiness with an inn-sign, however battered it may become, so her friends had learned to associate such pleasures with her appearance!) We find that we can occasionally modify our own behaviour or that of others by using appropriate reinforcements or aversive stimuli. Thus the theory appears to offer something of value to educators, even if the religious beliefs of some, and the earlier learning experiences of others, lead to rejections.

Questions

1. In social situations or in classroom situations how much can we learn simply by observing behaviour?

2. In what ways could behaviourist techniques be used to break a habit such as smoking? What circumstances might make this process difficult?

3. A child leaves possessions lying carelessly and untidily about the house. Which traditional methods are used to try to

change this behaviour? Which behaviourist methods might be used?

4. Does trial-and-error learning have any advantages? Should teaching always try to prevent the learner from making mistakes?

5. What are the advantages and disadvantages of setting behavioural objectives for teaching?

6. Which weaknesses in traditional school methods are indicated by behaviourist theory? Which traditional methods could be justified by behaviourist principles?

7. It is said that the hidden curriculum of schools conditions children to accept arbitrary divisions of time. How might it do so? What other conditioning can be attributed to the hidden curriculum of schools?

8. Why is large-scale 'social engineering' not possible at present? Would such engineering be desirable?

9. Which aspects of human behaviour do not seem to be well explained by behaviourist psychology?

CHAPTER 6

The curriculum for schools

Decisions about what schools should teach depend on what educators see as the desired result of education: but not all educators have the same opinions. Parents and education authorities may differ. Beliefs about the nature of human beings play their part. The child-centred educator will want children and their abilities to have a large share in deciding the curriculum while the collective educator will want to make sure that children learn the skills and the ways of behaving which are necessary to the life of the collective. We have therefore to look now at the variety of principles which determine curricula at present rather than at one particular theory of education.

One of the most frequent complaints in the history of education is that the present curriculum is wrong, that it does not prepare the younger generation suitably for life in today's society. Such complaints are probable because people tend to become accustomed to what they are doing: teachers especially are unlikely to ask whether what they are teaching has become irrelevant. We talk at times of education passing on the social heritage to the young: but in passing on a heritage there is always the danger of passing on some accumulated junk. Hence the need for critical inspection, from time to time, of what is being taught. To be critical, we need criteria; on what grounds do we decide whether subjects are suitable or no longer suitable? If the complaint is that some subjects are irrelevant to present-day society, this is already introducing the criterion that education should prepare people for present society: it is conceivable that it should rather prepare them to change it – or to maintain the values of a past society.

Another important question is to be answered: who decides the content of the curriculum? Some countries have a centrally determined curriculum, that is, the ministry of education or the government states clearly which subjects are to be taught at different levels and what the content of this teaching is to be: textbooks may be prescribed or may be chosen from a centrally approved list. In the United Kingdom such central definition of the curriculum has long been absent though religion has been officially prescribed. Yet the introduction of a core curriculum for England and Wales could be said to follow existing trends for in England the Department of Education and Science (for Wales, the Welsh Office), and the Inspectorate, publish discussion documents, guidelines and reports on the teaching of various subjects: in recent times also the Schools Council produced a number of publications on the teaching of individual subjects. In Scotland a Central Committee on the Curriculum produces reports on the curriculum in general, at primary or secondary levels, and on the teaching of individual subjects. In Scotland too a major Report[1] (the Munn Report) on the curriculum for pupils in the third and fourth years of secondary education has indicated a pattern to be generally observed. In both educational systems the recent introduction of the Technical and Vocational Education Initiative is a remarkable, centralised effort to change the secondary school curriculum by increased emphasis on the teaching of certain subjects.

External examinations and requirements to have various qualifications for entry into higher or further vocational education also standardise what is taught. They frequently decide what goes into the curriculum and which studies are regarded by teachers, pupils and parents as important.

Looking at contemporary criticisms and proposals raises questions: how did existing curricula come to be accepted and how are they justified? To some extent, it appears that schools simply go on teaching what has been taught, occasionally bringing in something new, revising a syllabus, or ceasing to teach some subject, and that this situation has continued for a long time. Such continuity is not necessarily a bad thing. It does mean that parents and children have some knowledge in common, having studied the same subjects, and parents can thus take a greater interest in what the children are learning. It means also that there is likely to be a good supply of teachers who are qualified to teach these subjects. When a system decides to introduce something new – as, for example, when Sweden decided to teach English in the primary school – it is difficult to find enough people able to teach this new part of the curriculum. There have lately been problems in finding school teachers of computer studies or craft, design technology: or, in some areas of Britain, teachers of non-European languages. These problems may be solved by conversion courses, in-service courses and other devices: but the process can be slow, especially as there is likely to be a strong rearguard action by teachers of the existing curriculum who see their subject threatened by the newcomers.

Schools and other authorities do from time to time ask if there is a need for change and state the principles which they think justify the inclusion or elimination of various subjects. These statements and existing curricula reveal conflicting theories of education. The DES, for example, has suggested that the

curriculum must prepare people for individual development, for work and for life in society. Are these the only criteria? Analysis of recent and earlier statements and actions shows that there seem to be seven principles referred to as justifying inclusion in the curriculum. Studies are intended:
1. to enable people to survive in their customary surroundings:
2. to enable people to earn a living or to follow a certain career:
3. to give pleasure:
4. to make good members of society:
5. to develop personal and moral qualities:
6. to give 'culture':
7. to develop the ability to think and to use knowledge.

These criteria are not necessarily independent. It is difficult, for example, to develop learners' ability to think and to use knowledge without also teaching them some knowledge or other. The teaching of subjects which give pleasure (a criterion not always recognised in curriculum planning) may very well contribute to developing personal and moral qualities and transmitting culture. Making good members of society presumably means also developing personal and moral qualities of the learners as well as teaching them to earn a living. Educating to give 'culture', which varies widely in definition and can be most controversial (e.g. the culture of the sciences versus that of the arts) may very easily include other aims. Yet these seven principles can be, and are, invoked independently, according to the educator and the society for which people are being prepared. Reviewing them we find conflicts, weaknesses and possibilities for development in what schools offer. They show that a number of decisions are to be made on more clearly defined principles if the present rather haphazard selections are to be improved.

BASIC EDUCATION

Teaching which enables individuals to survive in their actual environment is frequently regarded as the function of the home. There, certainly, we expect children to learn what to eat and what not to eat: to learn that fire burns: to put on or take off clothing at appropriate times: to observe elementary rules of hygiene. Some further teaching may prove necessary at school but this, like other basic education, may depend very much on the society in which the child lives. Information on how to cope with electricity, for example, or gas cookers, may be relevant in some environments but not in others. For parents in some societies basic knowledge may have to include knowing the signs of malnutrition or other afflictions of children or knowing how to prevent babies from dying from diarrhoea. In other societies children have to learn to avoid the dangers of alcohol, smoking, drugs: and this teaching has to enter the curriculum if it is not otherwise provided, though in the past it has mainly been left to agencies outside the school – temperance organisations, for example. Also for survival purposes, the curriculum at a later stage has to include information about venereal diseases and, to cope with recent dramatic discoveries, information about AIDS. Again, teaching of this kind has not always been regarded as a necessary part of the school curriculum, since other agencies have been expected to provide it. But the growth of some health problems and the realisation that school offers, in most societies, the one way of reaching young people who might otherwise not be educated in these matters has led to wider acceptance of the principle that the school curriculum should provide information necessary for the survival and health of the individual.

A part of basic education which has long been taken for granted is teaching the three Rs: this was seen as the basic function of schools when compulsory education was introduced. It is a provision for survival in societies which use communication by written words. It is assumed, despite evidence about fairly large proportions of adult illiteracy, that in modern societies people can, and should be able to, read and write. Research on illiterates has shown their difficulties: inability to follow written directions or understand signs indicating rooms, streets, dangers, instructions for use of machines or foodstuffs; deprivation in not understanding letters, including official letters; inability to read newspapers or other publications. It has however been argued that in societies where written communication is less used, learning to read has lower priority in the curriculum than learning about health and hygiene and food-growing. Spoken communication may replace written, e.g. in radio or television broadcasts or films. Yet the inclusion of reading in the basic curriculum continues to be justified even if there are good arguments for combining it, in some societies, with even more basic learning.

Similarly, the value of arithmetic has been queried. Its use in money calculations in everyday transactions is recognised, but it is suggested that modern calculators make the former well-drilled knowledge of numbers unnecessary. Elaborate calculations of compound interest, stocks and shares, areas of walls, capacities of baths, seem irrelevant to most learners in the school context. Even so, it is agreed that some knowledge of arithmetic has essential value: e.g. the individual should understand decimal notation, elementary statistics and at least be able to perceive when prices are inaccurately stated or a fading battery or error in using a calculator is producing incredible results. The value of skill in arithmetic for some vocational purposes is also recognised.

As for the third R, writing, it too has come under a cloud, especially if it is interpreted as hand-writing. It is suggested that developed societies have relatively little need for it. Communication can be achieved by telephone or by tape-recorder. If letters are to be written, they can be produced on the type-writer or the word-processor – and so be much easier to read (though access of many individuals to such devices is at times over-estimated and the need to insert in the curriculum training in such writing is often overlooked – typing has in some countries been dismissed as a vocational skill for girls, though keyboard work with computers is perhaps now changing that attitude). The place of hand-writing now seems to be justified in the curriculum only by a shift to another criterion, that of expression of individuality, or that of the aesthetic pleasure found in calligraphy. Writing in the wider sense, for communication of fact or fantasy, has had varying fortunes in the curriculum even if recent reforms have reinstated it as an activity to be cultivated in all subjects, not only in language lessons.

One notices also the gradual and unexplained disappearance from the curriculum of other aspects formerly thought basic. The teaching of accurate spelling, for example, was earlier regarded as part of reading and writing. It seems to have been much reduced because of reaction against excessive drilling methods in the past and some vague acceptance of the view that it is not a sign of defective basic education if one cannot spell correctly. Possibly, in an equally vague way, spelling is now regaining something of its former acceptance as an essential. The correct use of punctuation has followed much the same downward and now faintly rising trend. The analytic teaching of grammar has been a more openly discussed elimination from the curriculum, this elimination being justified mainly on the argument that it did not achieve its intended purpose of improving the individual's use of the language (One has to admit that the more recondite analytic exercises were probably beyond the understanding of large numbers of teachers also.) Here there is at times a revivalist movement from teachers of foreign languages who suggest that some modest knowledge of the function of words and structure of sentences is in fact helpful.

References to the place of language in the basic curriculum are sometimes obscure or misleading: they may fail to make it clear what is meant by 'the use of language'. Writing, we have noted, is important when it signifies the use of language in written communication. Oral communication, however, is also not always recognised as an important basic skill. It is sometimes assumed to be practised sufficiently in the ordinary exchanges of the classroom. Countries where oral examinations are customary are said to have an advantage here since in such systems pupils have to give, so far as they can, full and clearly spoken answers: in systems like the British pupils may find a laconic mumble suffices. Certainly many teachers in these systems have deplored the unwillingness of pupils to speak audibly – or indeed the unwillingness of some to speak at all when called upon to do so. Similarly, cultivation of the ability to speak in public, to convey information or a point of view to a group of people, has tended to be an aspect of the curriculum neglected in many schools or confined to school debating societies and those anxious to shine in them. Yet it is an important skill in social situations and important in education for citizenship.

As for the skill of producing the voice well, so that speech is agreeable to listen to – this again is said to be an area where some languages have natural advantages over others (English does not rank high in this respect). At any rate, this seldom is regarded as part of basic education, however basic it might seem. It tends to be included only in some schools, by some teachers: or by well-intentioned parents who pay for their children to have elocution lessons (which may not have quite the hoped-for results).

VOCATIONAL EDUCATION

If the criterion of necessity for survival gives rather unexpected definitions of basic education, showing it to be less universal and unchanging than might have been foreseen, many people would still argue that usefulness for earning a living is a major criterion or the major criterion. It is frequently said that many schools fail their pupils by sending them out unprepared to find and hold a job. Research on the opinions of parents and young people has certainly found that they think one of the school's main functions is to prepare pupils to get work. Schools and teachers have been accused of excessive devotion to fanciful ideas about education, promoting literature and other 'liberal' subjects at the expense of subjects giving usable vocational skills. The curriculum should therefore be more generally determined by the need to prepare young people for work.

The problem here is to know what a vocationally relevant curriculum would be. A number of arguments present themselves.

(a) The amount of preparation required for some occupations which employ large numbers of young people is very slight. It can be – and is, when some employments begin – given in a period of a few weeks. Specific vocational preparation would fill only a small part of even one school year. It can of course be argued that some 'background' subjects with a general relevance to work could be taught: but that brings in another criterion.

(b) If preparation for specific occupations is given this means that choices of future kinds of employment will be made while the young people are still at school. They may be still uncertain of their best choice. The school could find itself in the position of dividing the hewers of wood and the drawers of water from others if places were provided in certain courses according not only to interest but according to apparent abilities. (Largely to avoid this, reorganisation of secondary education in many countries during the last three decades has introduced comprehensive common schools to replace specifically vocational schools.)

(c) If schools are to give vocational preparation they must know which occupations will require workers in future and which occupations are dying. Pupils and parents may be naive about such things. In the past, for example, it has been often assumed that woodwork and metalwork had vocational usefulness for boys: many boys have thus thought they were being prepared to enter apprenticeships on leaving school and have been sadly disappointed. Similarly girls have assumed that typing gave an employment guarantee only to discover that other qualifications were required. Accurate knowledge of demands for workers with certain qualifications is hard to acquire, especially if the population is mobile. Thus general preparation to adapt to new skills and work seems the best vocational education to be given, if the curriculum can be designed to produce this flexibility.

(d) If criticisms voiced by employers are analysed, they concentrate more often on general education than on vocational preparation. Many employers, for example, complain of the young workers' lack of ability to use language well, lack of ability in basic skills, lack of ability to work with other people, poor attitudes to work. These complaints suggest wider criteria for framing the curriculum.

(e) Young people will not spend all their waking life at work. The school must prepare for social and leisure activities. This point, indeed, receives more attention now when unemployment figures are discouragingly high, especially for the young. Some critics suggest that the curriculum should be directed rather to preparation for unemployment – but this again raises problems of prediction and predestination. Which young people would have to be so prepared?

THE COMMON CURRICULUM

Since it is difficult to shape the school curriculum according to the future work of individuals, should we have a common curriculum for all? Historically, in secondary education especially, discriminations have been based on the social back-ground of pupils, on sex and on assessed differences in ability as well as future work prospects. These discriminations are now being eliminated: should they disappear totally?

The argument for the common curriculum is that if a subject is introduced for good reasons, all should have a chance to profit by it. All pupils should have basic education, subjects giving enjoyment and culture, subjects preparing for life in society, subjects training how to think. The only points for variation would then be subjects preparing for a specific occupation. Some countries try to avoid problems involved with specific training by providing 'polytechnical education', that is, an education which gives, not narrow training for one occupation or craft but under-standing of the scientific principles underlying modern methods of production and important in the living conditions of modern society. Such understanding might, Marx argued,[2] enable workers to transfer their skills more easily from one employment to another. It is also a kind of common cultural education, even if it is not always easy to put into practice.

Yet objections to the common curriculum have been raised. One, obviously a child-centred view, is that pupils should have freedom to choose. They should have a good range of options and be free to drop subjects which they find unattractive or unprofitable. (Various researches on pupil attitudes to school subjects have shown that pupils do make the distinction between liking a subject and thinking it useful.)

It has further been argued that we must allow for individual strengths and weaknesses so, again, pupils should be allowed to concentrate on subjects which they can do well and drop those they find difficult. Such thinking is evident in changes in various educational systems from giving certificates of complete secondary education only if passes in a set number and range of subjects had been achieved, to giving certificates for success in one or more individual subjects.

Various principles come into play here. It can be held that education should not reinforce inequalities in an individual's performance but should rather try to bring up to a more satis-factory level work which is rather weak. Is all-round excellence a worth-while aim? Admittedly, reasons for relative weaknesses have to be taken into account: they could be due to bad teaching – or to laziness in some areas where interest is not strong. While child-centred educators would support freedom to choose, others would argue, possibly for the good of society, that at least a minimum level of all-round competence should be aimed at. On the practical level there is also the question of whether learners can tell initially whether they are going to like a subject and succeed in it. Often a certain amount of work and time have to be given before reliable judgements can be made: hence an argument for maintaining the common curriculum for at least a substantial period of time. Knowing that certain studies are to continue may lead pupils to take them more seriously and so succeed. Granted, there is no hard and fast rule for deciding exactly how long a subject must be tried before valid decisions about liking it, or being good at it, can be made. The quality of teaching received is also important.

There is also the prosaic argument that the amount of time available is limited. If all pupils are to study a wide range of subjects, they will have relatively small amounts of the school week available for each. Consequently it may be difficult to reach the levels in some subjects which both teacher and pupil would wish – and institutions of higher education often set exacting standards of entry in individual subjects. Yet basic skills mastered in the primary school years still require maintenance and development. It may, however, be possible to adopt a cyclical approach, introducing a subject, leaving it out for a year or two, returning to it. Not all subjects have to be taught every year though some may need continuity if learning is not to be lost – foreign language study, for example, or some aspects of science or mathematics. Subjects may also be combined in various projects, without separate timetabling. In some systems it has been found that studies can be made through the medium of another language, thus making progress simultaneously in the language and in the subject. So adaptations of timetabling can make continuation of a large range of subjects more practical than might at first appear and some countries continue a common curriculum of a wide range of subjects into late secondary education, apparently without bad results. In France, for example,[3] pupils beginning upper secondary education have confronted a common core of French, mathematics, physical sciences, history and geography, a modern language and physical education in addition to groups of options: in East Germany[4] the upper secondary school class 11 has on the timetable German, Russian, a second foreign language, mathematics, physics, chemistry, biology, geography, history, civics and sport, in addition to options in practical work, art or music. Yet in other systems heavy demands made in some subjects or groups of subjects for entry to further or higher education still distort the curriculum. Teachers have to remind themselves and other authorities what the requirements for good education are and whether such education is compatible with early loss or abandonment of certain studies.

On the whole, the arguments for a common curriculum seem strong. They may seem to be challenged by current proposals for individualisation of the curriculum which would allow young people to have each their own programme of studies, possibly facilitated by computer programmes or other aids. Yet if certain studies are judged to have essential values, it is hard to support arrangements for some learners to avoid them. Individualisation of the curriculum could however be a useful development to allow learners to work at different levels and at different rates, according to interest at a given time – rather on Dalton Plan lines – and it could be useful in adding specialist subjects not included in the common curriculum.

STUDIES TO BE ENJOYED

It is seen as especially important to provide in a common curriculum some subjects easily dropped from specialist education. Child-centred educators have stressed the view that education should be enjoyable. Traditionalists tend to think that school subjects are there to be worked at: enjoyment is incidental or left to out-of-school activities or, possibly, to adult life once subjects have been mastered: or it may be asserted that any serious study produces enjoyment but that is not its principal aim. Yet a major reason for introducing the arts, music, dance and similar studies to the curriculum is that these are activities which human beings find pleasurable, and socially acceptable. They may, admittedly, also be justified as developing 'aesthetic appreciation' – which is, after all, a special kind of enjoyment. They may be justified further as a part of the cultural heritage, the knowledge which no well-educated person should be without. Yet if in school they do not give enjoyment, the teaching is failing of its purpose: no appreciation is being developed and the learners are unlikely in later life to continue such studies or even engage in conversations where their knowledge of the arts and music could serve as proof of a good education.

Some of these parts of the curriculum could be justified on alternative grounds: dance could be regarded as a contribution to physical fitness, for instance, or craft work could be seen as a practical skill. In some cases they lead to creative work to enhance the life of society: and they provide others in society with better understanding of the skill and effort demanded by creative work. They may also benefit society by enabling more people to discover satisfying ways of occupying leisure. But these subjects mainly claim inclusion because they are to be pursued with and for enjoyment, even if many teachers may hesitate to use this justification. There is possibly concern that teachers are not earning their pay if a study is simply for enjoyment, however socially acceptable.

THE DEVELOPMENT OF PERSONAL AND MORAL QUALITIES

Some subjects are proposed for the curriculum because they are also believed to contribute to the good development of the individual. Child-centred educators have justified the inclusion of the expressive arts also because such studies are believed to lead to better emotional development (this is a point to be considered later). More traditionally, the study of literature has been regarded as a means to such development. As the Bullock Report pointed out[5] in 1975, studying the works of great literature has been seen in Britain as a way in which the learner comes to understand human nature and so to empathise with other human beings. It provides, the Report suggested, reassurance as well as enjoyment. Great literature also, it has been argued, shows the good principles or follies of heroes and heroines, and their good or tragic consequences, so that moral judgements are formed and, presumabaly, acted upon. (Not all teachers of literature would accept moral judgements as an appropriate response to these works of art. This is indeed a point on which adult students and their tutors may often be at variance, but traditionally a moral emphasis has been evident both in the statements of intention by various writers and in the horror of some members of the public when literary works seem to them immoral.)

In something of the same way, the teaching of history was seen for some centuries as contributing to the moral development of the student by providing information about the lives of great men (almost exclusively, men) and the consequences of their wise or ill-judged actions. Even the fate of nations could be studied with regard to the morality involved.

The subject of the curriculum mainly expected to affect the moral development of the individual has of course been religion. As we note elsewhere, attitudes towards this teaching have changed and are changing. In some educational systems it is still seen as an obvious and essential component of the curriculum. In other systems it is gradually being replaced by some forms of moral education or by social studies. In others again, where religion has been excluded from the curriculum, some teaching of morality and/or out-of-class activities are expected to serve similar purposes.

Provision for teaching to develop the personal and moral qualities of the individual is not always a direct and overt part of the curriculum. Thus, while it may be expected that studies of literature, history or other humane subjects will influence personal development, as will religious education where it is provided – there is certainly no setting of behavioural objectives for these parts of the curriculum – personal and moral development may be expected as side-effects of the school's formal work, or left to school societies or youth or church organisations. Or it may be argued that the school's main contribution to individual development comes from the atmosphere of the school, the environment which allows for companionship and learning about social relationships, the discipline of the work itself and the standards of conscientiousness and honesty which it sets. Various writers, Paul Hirst among them,[6] have indicated the importance of the school environment and the need for fairness in its organisation if moral education is to be achieved. Such claims for the effects of school atmosphere are hard to assess in practice: but it probably is true that many educators, if not all individual teachers, believe that even if the curriculum does not explicitly include the teaching of moral values or personal development, the process of education will have a beneficial effect on moral and personal growth.

It is indeed argued that certain important attitudes and behaviours are 'caught not taught'. Hence, even if some 'subjects' are missing from the traditional curriculum, this does not mean that they have been overlooked or thought unimportant: personal and moral development is too complex to be directly taught. Yet possibly this belief is weakening in schools at present since many now offer counselling and guidance services which deal with attitudes and values which were formerly to be 'caught', or left informally to the help that concerned and interested teachers spontaneously gave to individual pupils. Scotland, for example, has a system of 'guidance teachers', members of the teaching staff who have special responsibilities and designated posts for giving help to pupils confronting personal problems of various kinds. Such provisions in Britain and other countries seem to indicate that the traditional curriculum has not always succeeded in providing for individual development – the weight of the opposing factors pupils may experience outside schools, in home life and the neighbourhood environment is now better understood, perhaps. Thus an additional service in schools tries to fill possible gaps in the curriculum.

Similarly, new courses in human relationships, in facing problems in the family and other situations, are now being formally introduced. Yet there is still some uncertainty as to whether such studies are properly part of the common curriculum – and whether enough has been done, as yet, to train teachers for such teaching. According to some critics, teaching here by inadequately prepared teachers can be disastrous (or simply boring): yet special preparation for such teaching is often not well provided – or not provided at all. It still remains unclear whether direct teaching is likely to be generally effective (though some pupils need and should receive individual, preferably expert, help). Do schools work most effectively for moral and personal development of pupils when an indirect approach is used? Has this point of view been taken to extremes and so requires modification by better planned additions to the curriculum?

MAKING GOOD MEMBERS OF SOCIETY

The 'caught not taught' argument has strongly affected much thinking in Britain about the aim of using the curriculum to produce good members of society. It has sometimes been believed that the traditional curriculum, through its teaching of religion, must make people behave well towards others and this has seemed a first essential of good citizenship. Knowing the history of the country has also been regarded as relevant since it should lead to better understanding of current events in society and thus to better citizenship, possibly even to better patriotism. Yet relatively little attention has been given in the British systems to explicit study by all pupils of the constitution or of the organisation of central and local government. Other countries give much more room to these formal studies in the common curriculum. Some clearly provide for the study of the basic political philosophy of the state, most notably for the study of Marxism-Leninism in the Soviet bloc. Others similarly try to ensure that all school children learn what are the major constitutional principles of their country. As we have noticed earlier, such teaching about political structures and duties may be part of the work of youth organisations as well as of school studies. In the United Kingdom, it is true, such organisations as the Scout and Guide movements have included statements about duties to God and the King (or Queen) in instructing their members, but such statements tend to be brief and their meaning not fully explicated.

Schools in different countries have also attempted explicit teaching about citizenship by ceremonies – reciting promises of allegiance or flag-saluting, as in the United States, for example – or by flying the national flag or displaying portraits of rulers or statesmen on the school premises.

Possibly differences between educational systems at the formal level are greater than at the informal level when education for citizenship is concerned. Certainly an international investigation[7] of civic education in a number of countries found some close correspondences in the views of teachers in these countries as to what characterises the good citizen. Being law-abiding and dutifully paying taxes received general approval but being a member of a trade union was something about which opinions differed. Thus proposals for civic education in the curriculum differ in different systems according to definitions of citizenship accepted by the education authorities of the country as well as according to their beliefs about how the behaviours and attitudes expected of good citizens can best be inculcated. As we have seen, countries with a collective system of education normally have clear definitions of the qualities of the good citizen and employ a variety of techniques in educating for citizenship – explicit teaching, group surveillance of behaviour, youth organisations, practice in conducting group meetings to discuss behaviour and performance. The content of subjects taught in schools is also used to inform learners about political policies and the duties of the good member of society. In other societies, much may be left to the discretion of individual schools or teachers, though societies with a central control of the curriculum include guide-lines to indicate what education for citizenship should be given and how, especially, attitudes favourable to the existing type of democracy in the country should be cultivated.

The British systems of education are probably among the most vague in their statements about this part of the curriculum. In discussion of suitable training for teachers,[8] the DES and Welsh Office did indicate that teachers must be trained to help pupils 'to acquire an understanding of the values of a free society and its economic and other foundations'. Other statements[9] indicated that teachers, as a result of their initial training, should have 'awareness of the ethical, spiritual and aesthetic values of society as well as its political, economic and legal foundations: respect for and understanding of the cultural heritage which belongs to the children growing up in our society: sensitivity to the diversity of cultural background in today's school population'. Such references to 'awareness' and 'understanding' may be intended to imply study in depth and a consequent determination to act on what has been understood but they differ dramatically from statements made in other educational systems about the need to develop in both pupils and teachers loyalty to the values of society, support for the principles on which society is organised and even patriotism.

Lack of specific definition may be a reason for the comparative neglect of education for citizenship in the curriculum in British schools, though it can still be argued that explicit teaching is often neglected because implicit teaching is thought more effective. At the same time there is an inherent unease in many liberal democracies about introducing politics into the curriculum. While some countries regard training in voting at elections as a necessary part of schooling, in British schools the running of 'mock' elections to illustrate the system and the views of different political parties has been regarded with suspicion by parents or local politicians. It is feared that such practices might be used to produce political bias in the pupils. Thus while the study of politics would seem a necessary part of preparation for citizenship, lack of trust in teachers' capacity to present such studies without attempting to influence pupils' views has considerably lessened the chance of such study being given an important place in the common curriculum. Again, one-party states have an advantage here since all teachers may be assumed to hold the correct political views. In many Western democracies, the teaching profession has tended to acquire, whether justifiably or not, the reputation of being left-wing in political views. There seems also to be uncertainty as to whether teaching about politics or even encouraging the young to become good citizens (a term admittedly needing thoughtful definition) must inevitably be undesirable 'indoctrination'.

At the same time, the curriculum in various schools in Britain now includes what are described as community studies. These vary in interpretation: sometimes they may consist mainly of visits to places of interest in the neighbourhood or surveys of conditions in the neighbourhood – industry, housing, leisure facilities. On other occasions they may be interpreted rather as service to the local community by visits to elderly people, or by work in gardens or other projects to improve the neighbourhood. It is usually assumed that such studies will develop not only knowledge of local society, and so help understanding of the larger society, but that they will produce feelings of solidarity with people in the community and so develop interests and attitudes which will make young people more concerned and active members of society when school years are over.

The curriculum in various countries has also been affected by another aspect of citizenship, that which attributes different roles in society on the basis of gender. So, in countries where women are not expected to be active in public life but are expected to confine themselves to serving their own families, school work differentiates. Boys are encouraged to study politics and to take part in discussions of such matters. Girls are rather allocated to home economics and carefully taught about the importance of the mother's role within the family circle. In some systems, for example in Saudi Arabia, these differences in interpretation of the citizen's role, mean that coeducation is regarded as unsuitable: segregated schools are preferred. In many other countries, however, schools have in recent years recognised the rights of women and men to equal participation in the affairs of society and have begun to remove from the curriculum any materials which could suggest otherwise: they have also tried to avoid earlier practices which made some subjects 'boys' subjects' and others, 'girls' subjects'. (This of course connects closely with the preparation for earning a living: vocational education is also part of preparing people to be good members of society.) In various educational systems girls have been found to be less well informed than boys about political matters,[10] possibly as a result of lingering beliefs about differentiated roles for men and women in political activities, though there is nothing to suggest that girls become less good members of society – on the contrary, perhaps. If active participation is necessary to good citizenship (this again depends greatly on the type of society for which education is preparing), further curriculum modification seems called for.

WORLD CITIZENSHIP

From time to time there have been proposals that school systems should look beyond national boundaries to prepare people to think of themselves as part of the larger society of nations. UNESCO especially has made considerable efforts to increase such teaching. In 1974, for example, it issued[11] a Recommendation 'concerning education for international understanding, cooperation and peace and education relating to human rights and fundamental freedoms'. Since this statement was endorsed by a large number of nations it might have been expected that the curriculum in various countries would be enlarged by appropriate teaching. Yet the movement in this direction has been sporadic. In England, for instance, the DES was 'confident that the response from this country will be shown to be both sympathetic and constructive' but also made it clear that no additional resources would be provided to help in following the Recommendation.

Possibly teaching for world citizenship is not a new subject but is to be achieved through the already existing curriculum. Certainly a number of countries have analysed the teaching of history in their schools and have amended textbooks and the syllabus not only to include a wider interpretation of history but to avoid nationalist bias. The Scandinavian countries, for example, have arrived at a common representation of their histories. Collaboration in research has attempted to harmonise French and German interpretations of European history (though the teaching of recent history still arouses considerable controversy in the two Germanies today). Information about international organisations and their contributions to world health, food supply and communications has increasingly been added to modern history teaching.

Similarly, in the teaching of science, the curriculum has sometimes been enlarged to show the contribution made by many countries to present knowledge and to show how scientific knowledge can be used for the benefit – or otherwise – of the world as a whole.

Geography equally can be taught to enlarge knowledge of the rest of the world and to develop understanding of the living conditions of people in other countries.

Literature, very obviously, can also enlarge appreciation of other nationalities and their way of life: so can foreign language studies.

In all these cases, and in the case of other common curricular studies, much depends on how subjects are interpreted and presented. Some countries have made considerable efforts to correct school textbooks which give misleading impressions about people of other countries. Some, e.g. Scandinavian countries, have encouraged textbooks even at the primary stage to include favourable references to people of other nationalities. Yet, very commonly, traditional syllabuses, concentration on external examinations – and the teachers' own knowledge of their subjects – mean that opportunities to teach to produce international understanding and sympathy are not taken. Further, in the British systems at least, many of these subjects become optional at quite an early stage: many pupils may therefore cease to benefit from them before they have had a real effect.

But possibly world citizenship also is better taught informally and through experience. School journeys abroad may contribute to international understanding, if they are suitably organised and more than a simple tourist excursion to enjoy sunbathing, leisure pursuits of various kinds, familiar food – and unfamiliar alcohol. Twinning with schools in other countries can create international understanding through exchanges of materials, information, visits by groups of pupils, as can arrangements for pen pals or individual visits to other countries. School projects, some organised by UNESCO, for aid to people in other countries have proved another way of developing international interests and feelings of mutual concern and friendship.

Individual school societies or membership of such organisations, in Britain, as the Council for Education in World Citizenship or the United Nations Association also help though these extra-curricular activities are likely to affect only a self-selected part of the school population. Similarly, youth organisations' provision of international contacts serve usefully for their own members. More general, if brief, interest may be evoked by special meetings in school time or by school observances of some ceremony on such occasions as United Nations Day.

In general it cannot be argued that preparation for world citizenship has become an important determinant of the curriculum – its inclusion might even be challenged by some parents and politicians – though some schools and some teachers in the United Kingdom and other countries have made admirable efforts to introduce this change.

THE CURRICULUM AND CULTURE

Here we arrive at a multitude of interpretations of 'culture' which affect the curriculum past and present. The old view, which Dewey criticised so effectively, was that some subjects, mainly literature and the arts, belong to and characterise a small elite group in society: such culture is regarded as available only to a minority who inherit the right to it or enjoy it because they have unusual intelligence or other talents. This view is not now advocated but survives, perhaps, in proposals for teaching the 'culture' of different groups in society – 'pop' culture, working-class culture, etc.

A more general interpretation is that some of the knowledge and skills which the human race has developed contribute so greatly to the quality of life that all children should have a chance to learn this knowledge and these skills. Most of the subjects traditionally taught in secondary schools are supported by such a belief. It is argued that children should at least be made aware of all aspects of this cultural heritage, even if it cannot all be assimilated during school years and even if it is difficult to decide what may reasonably be discarded. It is also emphasised that this culture is to be taught not only as knowledge but also for its effect on the attitudes and way of thinking of the learners.

This view of culture and its problems is discussed in many current writings by philosophers of education. Thus R. S. Peters has written[12] that 'Education suggests the initiation of people into what is worthwhile in a way which involves some depth and breadth of understanding and knowledge.' The effect of the studies must be evident in the individual's response to future situations: and culture here is widely defined as 'what is worthwhile'. Paul Hirst[13] has further developed proposals for the transmission of culture by affirming that there are distinctive 'forms of knowledge', having different concepts and being verified by different kinds of evidence. There have been variations in the listing of these forms of knowledge – one list included (a) empirical, (b) mental or personal – explaining human behaviour, (c) mathematical, (d) aesthetic, (e) religious, (f) moral, (g) philosophical forms: but the inclusion of a religious form of knowledge has been uncertain. It has also been questioned whether these forms are indeed distinct and unchanging (for example, it has been argued that mathematics has not remained the same kind of study during the centuries of its existence). Yet defining main areas of human interests – mathematics-science, history, aesthetics, religion: or physical-biological; humanities, social sciences; creative-expressive; moral; interdisciplinary – and proposing that children's education should introduce each of these is the method used by a number of contemporary writers on education: Hirst, Phenix,[14] Lawton[15] for example. The common principle is that certain areas are of major importance to human beings and a good school curriculum should provide learners with some experience of each of them.

It is not always clear how extensive this introductory experience should be. Many school curricula initially include some work in each of the designated areas but cease to provide for them all – for aesthetic subjects especially – at quite an early stage in secondary education. It is also not clear whether the distinctions between these subjects are as substantial as philosophical discussions have suggested: whether, for example, they do involve different kinds of thought processes or whether in, say, physical sciences and history, the need to find and respect all relevant evidence is the same, even if the kinds of evidence and the technical terms used are different.

The idea of developing 'many-sided interest' by studies in all major human disciplines is certainly not new. Widely educated writers on education naturally plan for others to enjoy what they have enjoyed. In the nineteenth century especially, the eminent psychologist and educator[16] J. F. Herbart put forward the 'many sided' aim for education, arguing that the individual was thus prepared to meet a wide range of situations and to react to them knowledgeably and morally. Even his classification of the traditional subjects was similar to many made today: he prescribed two main groups, knowledge interests and social interests, and in each a progression from immediate, specific data to general and speculative thought.

In such proposals for determining the curriculum there are four recurring problems.

(1) The 'forms of knowledge' approach tends to emphasise cognitive studies; does a curriculum based on them give adequate place to attitudes, relationships with others, citizenship? Much, no doubt, depends on the way in which they are taught.

(2) Do the definitions of the main areas indicate real differences or are they simply traditional? The contents of these areas obviously vary from one writer or one school system to another. Some specialists also complain that their own subject is unreasonably excluded, while others are 'smuggled into' a major classification. Foreign languages, for example, tend to be brushed aside as offering merely superficial or instrumental study: yet they have for long been regarded as of major importance and

would seem, in view of the increase in international contacts, to merit greater recognition.

(3) A practical problem is the response of learners. They, or their parents, may not be much impressed by a curriculum if, apparently, it is chosen simply to introduce all the main areas of human endeavour. The subjects offered must have intrinsic appeal or further justification. Of course, since they have proved satisfying to so many human beings over the centuries, they probably do have, if properly interpreted, continuing interest for people today: but this interest has to be made evident.

(4) The subjects defined as providing this kind of culture coincide largely with traditional curricula. Further justification of this definition may be found in the fact that so many countries agree in their choice of studies, including almost invariably maths, science, literature and language, history and, in most cases, religion. But these coincidences may show limits in our thinking. Are we unable to take an independent look at what should be taught or have we been conditioned to think along much the same lines as before? Changes admittedly occur, yet mainly as extensions of what is already there. Few curriculum proposals advocate radical change or a totally new approach. At various times innovators have proposed purely practical skills suited to modern society – learning how to use typewriters, telephones, domestic gadgets, cars, planes; studying space travel and astronomy: but these proposals generally fade away. There seems nothing comparable to the changes which, at the Renaissance, introduced the study of Latin and Greek masterpieces. Even the gradual introduction of scientific studies during the last century, while a marked change, does not seem to have produced a radically new orientation.

Defence of the traditional liberal curriculum may indeed be reinvigorated by critics when, as in Britain, government authorities are attempting to introduce considerable changes in the curriculum by the Technical and Vocational Education Initiative. Significantly, it is said, TVEI is controlled not by ministries of education but by the Manpower Services Commission and is intended to give greater emphasis to those aspects of the curriculum which are believed to have greater vocational relevance in today's society. It seems in many ways an attempt to reinstate the idea of a curriculum preparing for work, though the experiment was introduced with little systematic discussion of its principles. Yet as the content and organisation of the courses offered and supported by the extra funding differ from one local education authority to another, it cannot be said this is a systematic new approach, offering a reformed curriculum for all. Possibly some of the many evaluation exercises centred on the

TVEI provision will produce useful information as to young people's needs and responses in the favoured subject areas.

MULTICULTURAL EDUCATION

The demand that schools should provide multicultural education may also seem a proposal for radical change. It introduces another interpretation of culture: yet here also the definition of what is intended or wanted is not usually precise. Demand seems to centre on two main areas: language and the humanities. It is proposed that the curriculum should give a place to the home language of the various ethnic groups which constitute society. It is also proposed that the teaching of history should include the history of these ethnic groups and that religious, social and other studies should include their beliefs, their arts and preferred way of life. It is complained that schools focus on the culture, interpreted as the language, history, religion and customs, of the majority population.

The strength and emphasis of such complaints naturally vary in different countries today and also in different regions of individual countries. Much depends on the size of the minority ethnic group or groups in a given locality. Much also depends on the nature of the differences between groups – between immigrant groups themselves and between minority groups and the majority population. Probably, therefore, adaptations of the curriculum should to some extent be specific to areas of a country even if some general changes are made.

Adaptations in language teaching do seem to have to adjust to the local population. There are two main problems here: (i) enabling all citizens and future citizens of a country to use competently the official language(s) of the country and (ii) enabling members of groups who have a different home language to maintain and study their own language. The first of these problems becomes more complicated when a country has more than one official language: here it seems to be almost inevitable that children and their parents will use one of these languages rather than the other – as witness the precarious balances between French and English in Canada, French and Flemish in Belgium, English and Afrikaans in South Africa. The problem is further complicated if one of the official languages is a world language, thus having apparent advantages over the other 'minority' language. The availability of teachers of minority languages is yet another factor to be reckoned with – as in some of the smaller republics of the Soviet Union.

Much research in many countries has studied ways in which children whose home language is not that of the schools can be helped to achieve competence in using the country's language. (It has to be recognised that it is essential in any society that people are able to communicate with each other: hence the argument for all learning the official language – or the two or more official languages.) Controversy still exists as to whether it is better to adopt an 'immersion' method, accustoming the children to the use of the main language in ordinary classes, or to provide separate classes for them initially until they have become competent. In the former case, supplementary help by classroom assistants who speak their language seems desirable. In the latter case the danger of making the children feel stigmatised, or causing them to lose valuable parts of the ordinary timetable, has to be avoided. School help for children has also to be accompanied by evening classes for adults of immigrant groups. It is therefore a matter for local authorities to discover which language groups have to be helped and how children can best be assisted to acquire the necessary language skills.

Maintenance of the 'home' language leads to other kinds of provision. In the past, assimilationist policies have led to many immigrants losing their original language, or at least to its loss by their children, though their grandchildren have, in various countries, wished to recapture this lost form of identity. Much depends on the attitude of the parents – and of course also on whether immigrant groups plan to return to their country of origin. If parents want to maintain the language, they will continue to use it and so the children are likely to learn it. Parents may also decide to arrange independently for their children to study the language in out-of-school classes (this is of course more probable when the language, like Hebrew or Arabic, is related to religious observances). It would seem unwise to try to maintain a language which the parents are not interested in maintaining (the attempts in the Republic of Ireland to reinforce the use of Irish through the school curriculum have not been entirely encouraging; and the loss of Scottish Gaelic by many children and parents during the last two centuries, while encouraged by some schools, has been largely due to parental decisions). Consultation with parents thus seems essential here.

Further action to be taken by schools may still be hard to decide. The movement of populations in the world today means that a very great number of languages may be 'home' languages in any one country. It has been estimated that in Britain today over seventy languages are spoken. For the school curriculum to provide teaching in all the home languages presents tremendous problems of organisation and cost. For a foreign language spoken by a substantial number of pupils in any one area, local authorities can normally make provision for teaching through their schools, (if suitable teachers can be found), and speakers of the 'majority' language may also profit by this: yet many pupils in different parts of the country are likely to be in a minority too small for such provision. Here the solution would seems to lie in out-of-school study, correspondence or other courses, with audio and other aids. But there is also, for individual pupils, the question of reasons for choosing curriculum options in languages. In Britain the almost complete absence of teaching of non-European languages has been highlighted in recent reports. Pupils, however, also have to decide which language they consider most useful to them and their future; some may opt for a European language rather than their home language. Other pupils with a European home language may also choose to learn a non-European language if it is available. It depends, obviously, on their plans for their own future.

Provision for the religious and social beliefs of minority groups within the curriculum is still more complicated. We have noted elsewhere how parents' religious views are respected legally and how arrangements can be made for children to receive the desired teaching, even if such teaching is not always provided within schools. It is now argued in many places that religious education in schools should be general and include study of the major religions represented in the country's population. In Britain this is still an area where school practices differ greatly and where the ideal way of teaching about different religions has yet to be found. Whether school assemblies can offer services representing the religious groups of all children in the school remains uncertain; there is the danger of too great variety reducing interest and commitment. Possibly the solution of excluding all religious services from schools has something to commend it, since parents who have strong beliefs will ensure that their own children attend such services outside school.

Multicultural education has to cope with other complications in the form of dietary laws (affecting school meals) or religious holidays. Respecting the latter can disorganise timetables, even if in a minor way. Teaching about the traditional Christian holidays which affect the whole life of society in many European countries (possibly sometimes for commercial and practical reasons rather than from religious feeling) seems justifiable on practical as well as on other grounds: it can be accompanied by teaching about festivals of other religions, though this seems unlikely to have quite the same impact.

Teaching history and other humanities should present no great problems if the principles mentioned earlier of avoiding parochial or nationalistic interpretations are accepted. When it is a matter of cultural and social beliefs – e.g. about the freedom of the individual to make certain choices, or about the roles of men and women in society – then the curriculum may have to include both teaching about the principles which are generally accepted by society and indications that some groups within the larger society do not accept these principles. There is here a basic incompatibility which cannot be overcome: in multicultural societies, differences of cultural views occur: the curriculum cannot ignore these or offer the impression that all are equally accepted in society outside the school.

If principles of multicultural education are indeed to be used in determining the curriculum, some parents of the majority culture are going to be dissatisfied. They may claim that they like their own culture as it is and they see no good reason to modify and change it because people of other cultures have come to live in the same country. It is of course true that cultural changes have taken place for centuries because of immigrant or migrant groups and all cultures change to some extent as a result of interaction with others: but such changes have normally been gradual and often imperceptible, depending on the kinds of difference between newcomers and the indigenous population. If schools now inform parents that the curriculum is intended to give their children a new and different kind of culture, resistances and criticisms are inevitable – though schools could well propose, in according with existing traditions, to help pupils to understand people of different backgrounds better and to develop good relationships with them. It will indeed be a remarkable departure from the view that schools follow the wishes of parents and the majority in society if now the school curriculum is to be determined by a principle – preparation for living in a multicultural society – which is new, hard to define and contrary to many deeply rooted practices, beliefs and prejudices. The need for greater discussion with parents, and for a teaching profession that has thought out well the aims and intentions of the schools' policies, becomes greater than ever.

DEVELOPING THE ABILITY TO THINK AND USE KNOWLEDGE

We have finally to recognise this other principle for determining the curriculum. It can be expressed in its extreme form as asserting that it doesn't matter what we teach so long as it encourages the learners to think. More traditionally, we find it present in the argument that learning some subjects has transfer value, that is, the skills used in learning them are useful in learning other subjects or in other situations. For example, it has been argued that learning mathematics develops the power to think logically and that the study of Latin develops analytic ability or improves the use of the learner's own language. Many psychological researches indeed have been devoted to trying to assess the 'transfer of training' effect.

On the whole, results of such investigations have shown that the expected transfer does not occur. It has also been pointed out that this seems a roundabout way of teaching – why not teach people directly to use their own language well by teaching them that language? Some results however have suggested that if, in learning, we become aware of the techniques that we are using successfully, we may be able to use these general principles or techniques in later learning: and so there is, in a way, a transfer from one study to another. Present-day investigations of meta-cognitive thinking direct attention to this possibility of recognising the thought processes or strategies we are using and consciously using them on other occasions.

This view links with another popular view of the curriculum in recent decades, that it should concentrate on 'process not product' – that is, that the apparent result of a piece of learning may be less important than what has been learned *during* the learning. An extension of such thinking is that what the curriculum should mainly be cultivating is not knowledge but general learning skills. The survey[17] of primary education in England in 1978, for instance, emphasised the development of 'observational skills' or such skills as 'comprehension' or 'listening'. As Dearden has pointed out,[18] there is the danger here that we overlook the importance of what is being studied while such skills are practised: or that we come to believe that such skills can be acquired detachedly, irrespective of the material presented to the young. Similarly, perhaps, it has been asserted that knowing where information is to be found is as good as actually knowing the information.

While such side-effects of learning are undoubtedly important, it would seem that this principle of curriculum determination can be effectively used only in conjunction with others. Subjects indeed may be offered to the young for a variety of reasons, including their effect in stimulating observation and reasoning. But when subjects are advocated mainly or exclusively as a means of developing skills, their justification becomes suspect. Historically, it sometimes seems as though subjects which are on their way out of the curriculum are given a last-ditch defence by statements that they 'train the mind'.

In this respect we must recognise similar claims made for studies in higher education. It is at times pointed out complacently that graduates in certain subjects of study never use these subjects in their subsequent employment. Their studies have simply served to produce 'well-trained minds'. While it can indeed be hoped that all courses of higher education do cultivate such skills as collecting and assessing evidence and judging objectively with regard to all relevant and obtainable data, it must be hoped that studies which occupy undergraduates for so many months give them something more than these generalisable skills.

DETERMINING THE CURRICULUM

We have reviewed a number of principles which can be used to decide what is to be taught to the young. Evidently, some subjects can be justified on a number of principles: physical education, for instance, can be seen as contributing to the basic health and survival of the young, as a source of enjoyment (little as some school versions of the subject have lived up to this principle in the past), as preparing healthy citizens, or even as part of the cultural heritage of human beings. Some subjects are at present marginal, taught in some schools and in some countries (philosophy, psychology, for example): their justifications need further scrutiny. It remains a problem for educators to decide which principles are to be used for curriculum choices, to what extent and at what levels of education.

Decisions here will depend on the values held by the educator. Those who are child-centred will still look for guidance by what seem to be the interests of the young: Dearden in fact has proposed[19] attending to the 'needs' of the child, though again the definition of needs is not simple. Those who are oriented towards producing good members of the collective will attach greater weight to vocational and civic education. Those who cherish traditional values will emphasise the transmission of those subjects which seem to embody the most important achievements of the human race. Those with strong religious beliefs will propose a curriculum maintaining those beliefs and the way of life associated with them.

The decisions will also depend on the representatives of society and the resources which they think can be made available. The views of teachers in implementing the curriculum and in interpreting it – so far as they have freedom in their teaching – will markedly affect what is taught and, especially, which side-effects on thinking strategies and attitudes to learning it may produce. Hence the futility of imposing a curriculum or curriculum changes on teachers who are not convinced of the underlying values.

Ultimately, the success of the curriculum will depend on the receptiveness of the learners. Consequently we have to recall that it is not enough to decide unilaterally what is good for the young: if they are not motivated to learn, the schools' efforts are in vain. We have therefore, in making curricular decisions, to consider which principles are likely to produce a curriculum stimulating to the young, or how they can be convinced of the value of a predetermined curriculum. (The argument that this curriculum will lead to certificates necessary for employment or further education is probably not one to be recommended.)

Yet if the young are at times unappreciative of what schools offer, or if there seems to be too much to be taught, we can take comfort in the knowledge that education does not have to be crammed into a limited number of years. More and more people are finding satisfaction in studying at a mature age – indeed the 'universities of the third age' emphasise that education can continue life-long. In different countries, some adults are returning to secondary schools to pick up again the education they had not time for, or rejected, earlier. All kinds of provisions – study circles, societies, correspondence courses, distance learning, open universities, extra-mural lectures – exist to enable people to catch up with cultural riches or new skills, and to make their own curriculum choices. The actual choice of school curricula may be less vital than is sometimes assumed, provided that (a) the impulse to learn is not deadened; or (b) the collective encourages continuing learning and provides its members with the necessary resources; or (c) that people are conditioned to find learning a rewarding experience.

Questions

1. Consider any one subject taught in secondary schools today: what principles seem to you to justify its inclusion in the curriculum?

2. Why have the 'three Rs' been regarded as the minimum basic education?

3. What are the considerations which affect the place given to education for citizenship in schools in Western democracies?

4. Should subjects be included in the curriculum because they lead to enjoyment?

5. What seem to be the main problems in devising a multicultural curriculum? In what ways could these problems be dealt with?

6. What interpretations can be given to 'vocational education'? Is the principle of preparing young people for work a satisfactory criterion in choosing the curriculum?

7. What are the arguments for and against a common curriculum for all pupils in secondary schools, up to age 15–16 and up to age 17–18?

8. Which subjects, if any, seem wrongly omitted from the curriculum of schools today?

9. How do traditional curricula try to provide for the personal development of the individual?

10. Should the growth of adult education change our views of the appropriate age limits for compulsory education?

CHAPTER 7

Moral and emotional education

Many of the questions so far discussed have been concerned with the feelings of learners, with their attitudes towards learning and with their behaviour towards other people. Yet teachers may sometimes feel that their work should concentrate on cognitive learning only and leave emotions, attitudes and behaviour (outside the school and in adult life) to be dealt with by other people – by parents, for example, or by churches or youth organisations. Some teachers indeed are doubtful whether schools can have any worth-while effects on the moral and emotional development of the young. What are the reasons for this uncertainty and this unwillingness to be involved? Partly they come from awareness of the amount of competition schools face where morals and emotions are concerned: partly they come from the absence of clear theories of how education can influence these aspects of life. Moreover, there is conflicting advice about educating emotions. A. S. Neill asserted[1] that 'if you educate the emotions, the intellect will look after itself'. John Dewey wrote[2] that 'if we can only secure right habits of action and thought with reference to the good, the true and the beautiful, the emotions will for the most part take care of themselves'.

AIMS IN EDUCATING MORALS AND EMOTIONS

It is generally assumed that we know what the desired results of such education are: but although we can find many descriptions of the person who has received a good cognitive education, it is difficult to find a description in educational writings of the emotionally well educated person. Vaguely we think of such characteristics as 'balanced', 'mature', but it is not clear, for example, whether such a person experiences undesirable emotions but does not express them or whether good education means that undesirable emotions are not experienced in the first place. (Skinner was unusual in suggesting that the latter state could be produced by good education.) Similarly, if people are morally well educated, does this mean that they can form correct moral judgements or that their *behaviour* is always in accordance with good moral principles? The two do not necessarily go together – many people admit ruefully that they know what they ought to do but they just don't do it – yet presumably the educator would hope for both good judgement and good behaviour. How, too, do emotions affect morals? The commonplace experience we have just mentioned usually indicates that emotions prevent us from acting on our moral judgements. So how should a good education regard emotions – as something to be subordinate to moral judgements, especially when 'bad' responses should be avoided or at least not expressed, or as an aspect of human experience to be encouraged and allowed free expression?

When compulsory education was to be introduced in England, Herbert Spencer[3] was certain that it was unlikely to raise the moral standards of society and reduce crime. 'Whatever moral benefit can be effected by education must be effected by an education which is emotional rather than perceptive. If, in place of making a child *understand* that this thing is right and the other wrong, you make it feel that they are so – if you make virtue *loved* and vice *loathed* . . . if, in short you produce a state of mind to which proper behaviour is *natural, spontaneous, instinctive*, you do some good.' But, as he foresaw, the public educational system has not had these effects. Nowadays schools have to reconsider whether such moral and emotional education is something which can indeed be provided by them. Is emotional and moral education possible?

EDUCATORS' ATTITUDES TO EMOTIONS

It depends on how we view emotions. Their expression is certainly something which changes greatly from one age to another and one society to another. The dramatic expressions of approval and triumph on football fields today, for example, arouse conflicting responses among older and younger spectators: earlier they might well have been considered bad form. More generally, displaying personal grief in public is not generally approved of, though appreciated by some media representatives: there are also differences in what is accepted for males and females here, as there are differences in male or female overt expressions of aggression or fear. These social customs presumably reflect values set by society on various emotions.

Educators in the past have made it clear that there are good emotions and bad emotions. In Christian teaching and in the Ten Commandments some emotions are forbidden – covetousness, for example: teaching about the seven deadly sins focused, interestingly, on bad emotions, not simply on bad actions. Young and old were left in no doubt that they should avoid having these

feelings, let alone acting on them. Possibly succeeding generations have their own characteristic sins. Gluttony is less evident
in our health-conscious days and more likely to be interpreted
as a medical problem like bulimia. Avarice is little spoken of.
Sloth is perhaps becoming differently interpreted since the 'Protestant work ethic' has come under attack, though sloth seen as
laziness is still denounced in some sections of the population.
Envy continues to flourish, even, to judge by the literature, in
collective societies: the mass media may be charged with
fostering it. Pride is an emotion which modern society may find
it hard to classify as wrong yet, in some senses, it clearly leads
to bad behaviour today, as, for instance, in the arrogance of
some motorway driving. Anger and lust are possibly the sinful
emotions which most cause concern today, when anger can lead
to violence against people and property, and lust to rape, to
failure to form lasting relationships and to the spread of venereal
diseases among the whole population (even if, in some modern
interpretations, lust is not a harmful emotion but a natural enjoyment of sexual activities). In general, religious teachers, not only
of Christianity but of other major world religions, have given –
and some still give – a clear lead in advocating the elimination
or at least the control of some emotions. But the weakening of
religious teaching, and new interpretations of religious doctrines,
mean that teachers in schools, and parents, no longer have these
clear standards in dealing with emotions.

Other educators also have proposed the elimination or control
of certain emotions in the interest of the individual and of
society. Plato argued that tales of gods and heroes should not
show them indulging in bad emotions for in this way the young
might be led to develop such emotions also. Indeed, Plato would
have banished much poetry and drama from the ideal society
since these arts too often encourage enjoyment of emotions
which should be rooted out. In later centuries, under the influence of religious teaching possibly, John Locke set out[4] what can
be regarded as the Puritan ideal of the human being whose
behaviour is not controlled by emotions but by reason: children
'should therefore be accustomed betimes, to consult and make
use of their reason, before they give allowance to their incli-
nations'. Education thus should develop the habit of acting
reasonably and denying oneself emotional satisfaction or the expression of emotion if rational, moral judgement disapproves
such expression and satisfaction. This ideal has indeed been
commonly accepted in European education though the responsibility of achieving it has often been left to the home and the
church rather than attributed to schools.

Against this ideal, there has been a reaction in favour of
emotions and their expression: they are cherished as 'natural' and

as an important part of human personality. Possibly the diffusion of psychoanalytic theories has been influential here, though not only psychoanalysts have emphasised the importance of emotions as the driving force in human behaviour. Some – mistaken – interpretations of Freudian theory were that if the young child is not allowed to express emotions freely, this will lead to neurotic problems later in life. (Yet Freudian theory held that there must be a reconciliation or at least a compromise between the individual's pleasure-seeking drives and the demands of society. It was repression which, at an immature stage of development sent the wish underground, denying its very existence, that led to the later problems.) The extreme application of this 'theory' that denial of any of the child's emotional demands is hurtful to development, has had appalling consequences in many cases. Other psychological theories however have suggested that the dominating emotions of human beings could serve educational purposes. The love of dominance, which Adler singled out as the most important emotion (though this view was modified in his later work), could be used to encourage the young to achieve its satisfaction by excellent performance in one or other knowledge area or skill. Likewise psychologists have suggested that emotional impulses can be directed to new objectives: that aggression, for example, can be usefully turned to fighting against poverty and disease: or at least displaced and modified by expression in some forms of sport (rugby, for example).

DEFINITIONS AND CLASSIFICATIONS OF EMOTIONS

What is not clear, in existing psychological theories, is (1) which emotions the educator must expect to work with; (2) whether certain emotions will be found in all children; (3) whether there are natural stages of emotional development, just as there are physical stages of development and stages of cognitive development.

If we take the question whether human beings are born with an extensive range of emotions – aggression, fear, anger, love, acquisitiveness, for example – or whether these are simply names given to expressions and behaviours arising from only one or two innate emotions, we find conflicting answers. Freud, for example, narrowed the list to two, the pleasure-seeking and the death instinct. Adler, as we have just noted, suggested one ruling emotion, the desire for domination. Suttie[5] claimed that the basic emotion is to seek and enjoy security in the love and acceptance of other human beings and that behaviours of various kinds are adopted in response to the longing for this ideal situation (in his interpretation, a wish to return to a golden age experienced by the young baby, being admired and cherished by those around). Other psychologists have produced longer lists while others again have restricted themselves to a few basic drives – anger, fear, food-seeking, comfort-seeking. Anthropological studies have tried to discover whether some emotions are common to all human societies or whether some emotions which the observer might expect to be universal are not in fact present in some groups. Here it has been queried whether aggression is really an innate characteristic or simply a kind of response, in forms approved of by the society in which the individual lives, to frustrations of other emotions. War, it has been argued, is not based on an innate human characteristic of aggression: some human societies show no aggression and display instead emotions of cooperative, fostering behaviour. Names of emotions, some critics argue, are simply rather misleading labels which conceal a very small number of responses.

Even the nature of an emotional experience has been questioned. William James' theory[6] was that what we experience are physiological changes, stimulated by something in the environment or situation – changes such as an increased heart rate, blushing, quickened breathing: according to what the situation is, we interpret these changes as an appropriate emotion. This theory has been widely challenged; and experiments in giving people physiological stimulants to see if they then say they are experiencing an emotion have not really supported it. But part of this theory also suggests that if we 'go through the actions' of having an emotion, i.e. make appropriate changes in our physical state, we do indeed experience, or begin to experience, that emotion. Various modern methods of role-playing and expressive movement do tend to support this view. (An extremely simple form of it is the advice to smile – or keep a stiff upper lip – to change one's emotional state for the better. Similarly teachers frequently read from physical signs information as to how pupils are feeling about their work and try to change pupils' attitudes by telling them to change their posture, e.g. to sit up straight.)

We remain at the stage where, despite various psychological analyses, we are not quite certain whether certain emotions are innate (interest in other human beings might have been claimed with certainty to be the one universal emotion were it not for observations of autistic children who apparently do not all experience this basic emotion). We are also not quite certain how we discriminate among our emotions – if, indeed, we can reliably do so – or whether we simply provide an appropriate label as our social experience has taught us to do.

It is also not clear whether we pass through stages of emotional development. The Plowden report certainly seemed to suggest such a progression, certain emotions being experienced and having to be controlled in the early years. Erikson has suggested[7] rather that at different stages during human life there are dominating emotions and the good development of the individual depends on whether, at each stage, the positive rather than the negative emotional pole is chosen. Thus, successively, good human development depends on the coming into prominence of the following emotions, each at the appropriate period in life: trust; autonomy; initiative; industry; identity; intimacy; generativity; ego integrity. These emotions remain through subsequent 'ages' and, as the list will indicate, the final stage of ego integrity is attained only late in adult life. This classification has seemed satisfactory to many people, though it is not supported by extensive research evidence. It could be argued that it indicates simply the emotions likely to be elicited by the different situations individuals meet with as they become older and mature into adulthood: it does not necessarily indicate that these emotions would develop in the same sequence without the given pattern of social situations. Nor does it indicate that the emotions themselves change as the individual grows older even if a chosen pattern of emotional responses is adopted.

One notes also that various cognitive elements enter into the situation: the 'ages of man' are not a purely emotional progression: ego integrity in particular subsumes a great many cognitive experiences. Similarly when Krathwohl, Bloom and Masia[8] suggested in their *Taxonomy of Objectives – Affective Domain* a series of affective stages paralleling the developments in cognitive thinking, this series also included various cognitive elements and scarcely corresponded to 'emotions' as commonly understood.

We come to the view that whatever the nature of emotions they are unlikely to exist without interaction with cognitive thinking. Even theories about the benefits of the expressive arts in good emotional development indicate that in attempting to express emotion through the arts the individual has to become aware of the characteristics of the emotion and the characteristics of the medium of expression and work to reconcile these, i.e. it is not a case of experiencing emotion alone: there is an important element of reflective thought. In various forms of psychotherapy similarly, undesirable emotional reactions are modified by techniques which produce cognitive insight into the emotional problem: client-centred therapy, for example, leads the individual to think out his or her own interpretation of the problem and its solution. Education has therefore to decide how the interaction of emotion and cognitive thinking is to be cultivated in moral behaviour. It has to consider also how far some emotions may be enjoyed for their own sake if they are not incompatible with moral judgement and conduct. This is what is meant by talk of educating the emotions. Emotions themselves seem ineducable: educating them is a matter of integrating them with cognitive controls. It is thus difficult to see how emotions can be, as one Report put it, 'exercised' in the sense of becoming stronger and better. They can be given variable amounts of opportunity for expression certainly: but there is much to suggest that the emotion of anger, for example, remains essentially the same from early childhood to full adulthood, although modes of expressing it become more subtle and the adult has greater opportunities than the child to change situations which arouse this emotion.

EMOTIONS IN SCHOOL

The experience of school life will inevitably include various emotions, some deliberately stimulated, others unintended or not noticed. The curriculum itself does try to arouse various emotions of pleasure, by its inclusion, as we have noted, of art, music, dance, crafts, literature. Other school subjects in themselves can produce pleasing emotions: for example, some people delight in the elegance of a mathematical solution: for others, there is the enjoyment of the qualities of words and their ordering. Even the neat and precise setting out of work can arouse pleasurable feelings in its creator (just as the mere appearance of badly written, scruffily presented work arouses not only a cognitive disapproval in the viewer).

In general also, the school situation can give rise to positive emotions when the individual feels a sense of achievement, in any school work. Here the findings of observers about the proportions of praise and blame in teachers' comments are obviously relevant: even if very little emotion may be generated by any one such comment, the cumulative effect can have a marked effect on the emotional state of the individual.

Much less obviously too, the school environment, as we have noted, may be such as to produce a positive feeling of pleasure and well-being, or a mood of depression and discouragement. In England a recent inspectors' report on the conditions in which A-level classes were working commented on the shabby and disagreeable surroundings of many such groups.

Also difficult to calculate and control is the effect of the social life of the school. For many pupils, meeting friends at school is a positive emotional satisfaction – for some, the only satisfaction school offers. But the relationships generally prevailing in the school, its organisation and discipline also affect the emotional state of both staff and pupils.

Thus, apart entirely from attempts to introduce cognitive interactions with emotions, schools do affect, through the formal curriculum and through the general atmosphere and environment, the emotional states of their pupils even if this is not seen as education of the emotions.

MORAL EDUCATION

When we come to the question of affecting emotions so as to produce good moral behaviour and moral judgement, we find inevitably some other major problems – in addition to the difficulty of the task itself.

A major problem is the definition and justification of the moral standards which we hope the young will adopt. There was much less of a problem here in the past when religious education offered clear definitions and direction. In many societies today moral education is still based on specific religious teaching, as, for example, in Iran or in Saudi Arabia where the doctrines of Islam provide definite moral standards for all the population. In many other societies, however, the population is not united by a common religious belief: where a specific religion is said to be accepted by the majority of the people, as Christianity is in many Western countries, there may still be considerable variations in the interpretation of that religion – as, for example, between Roman Catholic and Protestant churches: or, more importantly, many of the population may simply be apathetic with regard to religion. In Britain, for instance, the proportion of people regularly attending the various Christian churches is remarkably low: and public opinion surveys often show that what the majority retain are simply a few rudimentary beliefs in the existence of God or Christ and the use of prayer.

Religious education and moral education are of course not necessarily linked together, even if most world religions do provide moral guidance for their adherents. But if religion is not offered as the origin of moral teaching, difficulties arise. Religion has the prestige of divine origins. Its 'laws' are not the expression of the ideas of human authorities, they claim divine authority. Disregard of these moral teachings is expected to lead to punishment, now and/or in an after-life: and these undesirable consequences cannot be evaded by concealment, since the divine power cannot be deceived. Thus religious teaching which is believed by parents and children does enjoy the benefits of tremendous authority in setting moral standards: it makes clear to the younger generation (as to adults) what they should or should not do, why they must control certain emotions and how they should interact with other people. Further, in the society where one religion is accepted by the overwhelming majority, moral education given by home and school will be in harmony.

In theory at least, young questioners will meet with the same response from all authorities: and they cannot hope to evade the consequences of their misdeeds, or even of their wrongful feelings and thoughts.

JUSTIFICATIONS OF MORAL STANDARDS

The situation obviously is different when the questioning by the young: 'Why *should* I do that – or not do that?' cannot be met by reference to divine and immortal teaching. To some extent, however, it can be met by reference to the views of people in general: and this is much more likely to be effective if there is what could be described as a strong social consensus, that is, if most members of society do hold the same moral standards and there is some public expression of these standards.

We can see examples of this kind of foundation for morality in one-party states where the political orientation of society will entail certain forms of behaviour and will authorise or forbid certain kinds of action. To a great extent, collective education relies on a strong social consensus as the basis of moral education. The needs of the collective demand cooperative behaviour towards others: they may also require loyalty, criticism in public of any antisocial behaviour and, allied to this, self-criticism where the norms of the collective have not been adhered to. Certainly, collective education states clearly for the young how they should behave. The sanctions for 'bad' behaviour are also clear – they consist in public criticism, possible mockery or humiliation, expulsion from the group, exclusion from the benefits which the collective gives to its members. Again, there is likely to be agreement between home and school authorities as to what the expected standards are. There may even be re-inforcement by the peer group of the moral teaching given by adult authorities. The reasons given for the moral standards to be followed will be that this kind of behaviour is necessary if the collective is to survive and prosper: and that other people will not be friendly and helpful unless the child or young person behaves in the approved way. It is normally assumed that the need for the collective to survive and prosper is self-evident: certainly the need to avoid being a social outcast is strong.

Justification of moral standards is less easy in societies where social consensus can be described as weak and where many opinions are expressed as to what constitutes acceptable or right behaviour. The Danish Council planning for education at the end of this century did suggest that there were in Danish society certain moral concepts which could be regarded as generally acceptable – the Council listed[9] such things as not telling lies (though 'white lies' might be permitted), keeping promises, respecting the rights of other people, not taking the law into one's own hands, not using violence. In fact, in Western democracies, such principles would be almost universally agreed. The difficulty is that some of them may fall out of favour or may be argued against by some sectors of society (not taking the law into one's own hands, for example) and that there seems to be no central authority which clearly states these principles. The present discussions about AIDS illustrate the problems of finding general authoritative statements on morals. Sexual promiscuity is seen as involving practical dangers, and ways of avoiding these are clearly publicised. Yet most authorities, even including some church authorities, seem to hesitate to refer to moral considerations: and statements by some young people (and others in the community) show that they see no moral issue here since their education has left them confident that people have a right to uninhibited enjoyment of sexual pleasures. There is no social consensus on any moral standards involved here and so no clear statement on this aspect.

It is probably in questions of sexual morality that we find today most of the 'grey areas' in societies where social consensus is weak. It is also true that in these areas, the acceptance of principles may change within a decade or two and may vary from one part of the country, or one social group of the country, to another. The attitude towards unmarried mothers is a case in point. Since it has been commonly accepted that the moral lives of teachers must be beyond reproach (teachers being expected to set an example to the children, even if the children's parents do not always set such an example), until recently it has been assumed that an unmarried woman who has a child is morally blameworthy. But the policy of local education authorities in this matter now varies in England, some happily accepting the unmarried mother as teacher, others requiring that she resign. Similarly, some authorities accept that a teacher may be cohabiting without marriage, while others would not appoint or at least would not promote such a teacher. In France, during the 1970s, there was an interesting illustration[10] of varied and changing attitudes in such matters when a young woman teacher, who had been cohabiting, evidently without attracting official disapproval, decided to have a child. There was a call, partly from parents but also from some teachers of the area, for her dismissal. (It was argued that she would deter parents from sending their children to the school where she taught and this school would thus lose numbers in its rivalry with a neighbouring church school.) But the Ministry of Education, on this occasion, upheld the right of the unmarried mother to stay in her teaching post.

A similar difference of views, differently resolved, has been evident with regard to teaching about homosexuality in English schools. When a London area authority was apparently presenting as acceptable[11] the situation of a small girl being brought up by two male homosexuals, there was considerable objection by parents and others and the Secretary of State for Education was ready to ban the offending book. Similar attempts to present homosexuality as acceptable and indeed normal have elicited strong protests from parent groups in the areas in question and have been abandoned or modified. Yet, and this also illustrates the problems of social consensus, opinion polls among teachers[12] have shown that nearly half of those studied were not sure what their own view was concerning teaching about homosexuality. The homosexuality of some teachers also affects the situation.

In Britain, attitudes seem to depend greatly on the area where the school is situated and the extent to which parent groups may object to, or accept this preference of the individual teacher. Much depends also on whether society claims the right to set standards of behaviour for teachers or accepts that the private life of teachers is a matter for individual teachers alone. Again, the school policies depend not on a general social consensus but on what is apparently the general consensus within the local area. Yet this adaptation must reduce the amount of agreement in the moral standards set before the younger generation as a whole, although it can be claimed to give greater freedom to individuals who can move to an area in sympathy with their views and so allow a wider choice of life-styles in a society.

There are of course other aspects of moral behaviour where grey areas exist and where teachers may differ from their colleagues in deciding what standards should be set. Attitudes to shop-lifting have been known to vary, some teachers being inclined to regard the practice as endemic to the school neighbourhood and the pupils' way of life while others try to root it out. (Theft within the school is likely to meet with common disapproval.) Similarly teachers may differ – in their beliefs as in their own behaviour – about the need to develop honesty in relations with other people and the desirability of working conscientiously.

RATIONAL JUDGEMENT AS THE BASIS OF MORALS

If religion and social consensus are failing to provide justifications for moral standards to be accepted by the young, and in society generally, there remains the possibility of referring to the use of reason. While no societies at present can be said to exemplify this form of moral standards, it is firmly held by many educators that the ultimate goal of education is to produce the rational, autonomous individual, one whose actions are based on acceptance of general moral principles which reason can discover. This form would be superior to other forms of moral education since behaviour would not depend on external or distant sanctions and there would be agreement among all the educated as to the moral standards to be accepted. (It is assumed here that the use of reason will lead to common moral principles: this assumption is debatable. It can also be queried whether this view overestimates human capacity to reason. Yet few alternatives to this theory hold promise.)

There are certainly some doubts as to whether all human beings, at all ages, are sufficiently intelligent to reason out correct moral judgements: though here it can be said that the kind of judgement to be made is usually proportionate to the abilities of those concerned – children, for example, can show very good judgement in dealing with the practical moral problems which may confront them. Even so, it is sometimes suggested that there might be a need for a kind of interim moral guidance for those who have not yet reached the stage of abstract reasoning or who do not reach it in maturity.

STAGES OF MORAL DEVELOPMENT

There is widespread acceptance of the view that moral judgement does follow distinct stages of development. Piaget indicated[13] an evolution of the child from the stage of being self-centred to the stage of recognising the rules and rights of other people to the stage of making the individual's own rules. The theory of Kohlberg,[14] which has aroused interest in many countries of the world, also indicates stages of development, from the first stage of personal responses – believing that what is punished is wrong and that what gives personal satisfaction is right – to a stage where it seems important to gain social approval by doing what people expect (being a 'good boy' or 'nice girl') and, further, recognising that society has rules which are to be obeyed: the next stage is that of recognising the need for some kind of social contract which determines the behaviour of members of society, and, at a still higher level, recognising universal ethical principles which should determine behaviour. The definition of the various levels and stages has varied from time to time and there have been suggestions that possibly there is a still higher stage of development, rarely attained and therefore hard to describe.

While Kohlberg's theory has been supported by a considerable amount of cross-national research, there remain uncertainties as to whether this is a finally satisfying account of stages of moral development. The possibility of regression to an earlier level is admitted: people may judge at different moral levels, according to the situation. It has also been pointed out that women tend apparently to reach generally lower levels of moral development than men on this scale so it has been queried whether there is some built-in sex bias in the problem situations which are used to elicit moral judgements or in the kind of judgement chosen for assessment. (There seems no *a priori* reason that women should be less good in moral judgement than men.) Moreover, somewhat depressingly, it would appear that the majority of the population, male and female, do not advance beyond the middle levels where social approval for their behaviour or the formally existing social conventions are seen as the ultimate criteria.

A major weakness of this view of stages of moral development, so far as educators is concerned, is of course that while people may give admirable reasons concerning the morally right action to be taken in a hypothetical situation – fascinating as some of the test situations are – there seems no necessary link between the ability to reason well here and the habit of acting on similarly good moral principles. It has been argued that various law-breakers and delinquents are very well able to perceive and state the moral as well as the legal principles against which they have acted. Even so, the theory is useful to educators in indicating to them how thinking about morals may develop in children.

METHODS OF MORAL EDUCATION

If schools are to be concerned not simply with progress in thinking about morality but with associating moral judgement with moral behaviour, methods which are proposed to do this demand attention.

Theories of progress from one stage of cognitive development to another suggest that movement onwards can be stimulated by the environment. In the case of developing moral judgement, hearing the views advanced by those at a rather higher level is said to stimulate movement to the next stage. Such stimulation is sought in various methods of moral education. In practice, the most common approach is to use group discussion, possibly supplemented by dramatisation of relevant situations, or by the study of films, pictures, documents which present facets of an issue on which moral judgement is important. This approach supersedes former methods in which moral principles were simply taught to the young by stating them and having them repeated or written; or, possibly, by illustrating them by appropriate stories or fables. When morality was presented as originating in religious teaching, then, naturally, it was linked to study of the

Bible or other religious books. But there has been also, as we have noted, an indirect approach through the teaching of literature and history (with discussion of people's behaviour). More particularly, there have been attempts to teach through stories of heroes or heroines, whose example and principles the young might learn to follow: children's literature of the late nineteenth and early twentieth century includes some highly attractive – and apparently effective – works of this kind, even if their effect is restricted to children who read with ease and enjoyment.

Probably the most popular approach at present is that described as the values clarification method. Here, using various stimulating examples, the group is led to develop skill in discriminating among statements of fact, of opinion, of values: to become aware of relevant data and to seek for as much relevant data as possible: to become aware of the different values which people may hold with regard to the issue being studied. In this way, individuals are enabled to work out what their own values are, to choose values in awareness of alternatives, to affirm and maintain their chosen values – and, it is hoped, to act in accordance with the values they have chosen.

Evidently, this method demands the kind of rational thinking which has been regarded as the best foundation for morality. Equally too, a great deal depends on the atmosphere in the group. If the teacher tries to pre-determine the conclusions reached, then the method is not being properly used and no lasting effects on the learners are to be expected. Similarly, attempts by some group members to force their conclusions on others have to be countered by insistence on using the method properly – attending to relevant data, which the dominating people may be overlooking, for example. There must also be protection of individuals' rights to express their views without being mocked or shouted down by others. The atmosphere must be one in which reasonable discussion is possible for all. At the same time, the fact that these discussions are carried out in a group setting probably makes the conclusions more memorable and more likely to be acted on than if the study were carried out individually: awareness of other people's views and knowing that they share the same values have been shown to be effective in determining behaviour: so this method does have emotional components.

THE NEUTRALITY OF THE TEACHER

To use the method successfully, the teacher must avoid imposing his or her own views on the group: teachers are sometimes said to find this difficult. But the emphasis laid on the teacher's role of neutral chairmanship by Lawrence Stenhouse[15] and others has caused disquiet among many teachers. Neutrality has to be correctly interpreted. Most would agree with Paul Hirst's view[16] that it is a 'travesty of education' if the teacher remains inactive while pupils go on expressing ignorance and prejudice: no good moral education is likely to result from such a situation. The situation can be even more difficult where strong social tensions affect the classroom situation, as, for example, in the work of a Northern Ireland curriculum project[17] where a teacher reported great unhappiness about a class discussion in which one pupil was trying to dissent from the view of the others that all Protestants are bad: she argued that in times of illness in her family, Protestant neighbours had been kind and friendly. Yet her classmates were ready to cite many instances of hostile behaviour to them by Protestants. The pupil expressing a minority view obviously suffered from the reactions of the rest of the group: yet the teacher, having been told to be a neutral chairman, did not think that intervention to help her would be legitimate. In this instance, neutrality was being misinterpreted: the chairman should have insisted on better application of the techniques and skills of discussion. Yet the effectiveness of such insistence would depend greatly on the earlier introduction to these skills and success in making the group willing to use them.

This example is particularly useful in recalling that moral education in schools does not begin with a clear field: frequently, it is a matter of getting rid of existing prejudices and errors. It also emphasises the need for teachers to be adequately prepared to use such methods and to exercise judgement as to the way in which the discussion is developing. It is too often assumed that anyone can run a group discussion and any teacher can teach moral education: in reality careful preparation is needed so that teachers are clear about their own values and understand correctly what kind of discussion is likely to have benefits in forming pupils' values – and to what extent their choice of materials may pre-determine conclusions.

THE CONTRARY EFFECTS OF THE MASS MEDIA

In group discussions, references to the mass media, especially to television, are likely. Existing prejudices and errors in children and young people's moral standards are very often attributed to the continuing and insidious effects of the mass media, television in particular. Moral education in schools has therefore to decide how to cope with the opposition, if indeed there is competition here.

It is true that for a very long time educators have worried about the effects of the media on morality.[18] Plato denounced theatrical performances: so did the Puritans. As books and news-papers became more widely available, so fears grew that reading them would corrupt the morals of the population. It was not only a fear of political subversion that led to restrictions on publi-cation of newspapers and other works but a concern about morality which, later, led to restrictions on the number of fictional works that a reader might borrow from public libraries at any one time. (Until quite recently, in various parts of Britain, readers' tickets carefully discriminated between fiction and non-fiction works – though works in a foreign language did not necessarily count as fiction, since, presumably, reading them demanded a safe-guarding effort.) Later, radio broadcasts were seen as a threat to the minds of the young; then films were the greater danger, then horror comics and, eventually, television and video nasties. Thus the history of popular education and the media shows a continuing concern about possible corruption, the concern shifting to what seems to be the most influential contemporary medium reaching the masses. Whether this indicates the need for continuing vigilance or an underestimation of individuals' ability to resist such contamination is uncertain.

Unfortunately, the precise effects of the media are hard to measure and hard to prove. Many researches have attempted to discover whether there is, for example, a link between much viewing of television and violence by young people. The link is difficult to establish, since so many other variables intervene – the actual circumstances of the viewer, reasons for extreme amounts of viewing, the possibly contradictory effects of other television programmes, the length of time during which the effect of a television programme is likely to last. (Admittedly, the cumulative effect of many similar programmes may be less easily forgotten or cancelled out than the effect of any one programme.) Results are by no means clear-cut. Actual effects on behaviour seem difficult to prove, though there are occasionally spectacular cases where viewing of violent action is said to have been followed shortly by engaging in similar violence in real life – such instances of course tend to make us forget temporarily the many thousands or millions of viewers who are not stimulated to such action. Certainly, some research has also indicated the insights which viewers develop from a young age, their ability to discriminate among different levels of reality, and, in adolescence, their growing, sometimes cynical, awareness of techniques of advertising which are calculated to influence them.

CENSORSHIP QUESTIONS

Although stimulation to specific actions is hard to prove, it is evident that the mass media do produce imitation of styles of dress and manners. There seems to be also some assimilation of the values most commonly implicit in the media. Hence there is the recurrent question of censorship to protect the morals of the young, and even of the adult, population.

In some ways, it seems simple to ban broadcasts, books, papers or periodicals which include materials likely to have a detrimental effect on morals. But immediately there is the question who decides what is to be banned. In collective societies it may be possible to find a group of people who are accepted as satisfactorily representing and applying the judgement of the society. In societies with a variety of standards, this is not easy – as many debates about the action of censors regarding films or books have shown. (Decisions about banning may of course be taken not for moral reasons but for what are believed to be national security reasons: the principle of finding people whose judgement can be generally accepted remains the same.) Again, while the explicit content of books, plays, films, etc., can be judged, it would be a very difficult task for censors to decide which attitudes are being promoted by values implicit in the content.

Much depends also on willingness to accept censorship. Here the problem is compounded by the fact that the mass media reach all levels of the population, old and young, well educated and uneducated. The use of Latin in times past and, possibly, of foreign languages in the earlier British libraries, seems to be a rare instance of a method by which communications will reach only those judged capable of receiving them safely. Thus adults who might agree to some censorship of what children view will resent censorship which allows them to view only works judged suitable for children. (The time barrier, assuming that children do not view late in the evening, has proved largely ineffectual.) There is also the general democratic argument that free citizens should be allowed to judge for themselves what is or is not good for them.

One major argument against censorship is that it is almost impossible to apply it effectively. Admittedly it is easier in countries where there is state control of publishing and imports: but even there, determined people do, to some extent, obtain access to censored materials. (Granted, the less determined will remain unaware of what has been censored.) In domestic circumstances, it is, in most modern societies, difficult for parents to exercise complete control of what their children read, listen to or view. Parents may certainly decide not to have a television set in the house (they are a very small minority): they may rule against viewing after certain hours or against viewing certain programmes: they may refuse to have certain books or papers in the house. But if the children are in contact with other children then they will learn about what their parents have censored and may view, in their friends' houses, what their own parents would not allow: or they may read friends' copies of banned literature – or even read it in the school or the library. The only effective safeguard here is the child's acceptance of the parents' view and willingness to abide by their judgement.

Schools similarly cannot control which programmes pupils watch or listen to or which books and papers they read. Certainly, the school can censor its own teaching materials or library stock and may sometimes, through parents' representations, be brought to discard some books or materials: it can also advise against or denounce some books, magazines or programmes. But since pupils demonstrably spend much time attending to television (though the quality of that attention is not always certain – much 'viewing' may be absent-minded) teachers in schools may well feel that the morals of pupils are going to be determined more by these uncontrollable out-of-school influences than by what is offered or recommended in school. Popular programmes have so much more glamour and prestige (in the eyes of pupils) to reinforce their messages that the school's impact appears relatively feeble.

What can be proposed here, for both parents and teachers, is a kind of indirect censorship or at least the use of counter-attractions. Good examples of books, films, programmes, can be introduced so that the young form their own standards independently in reacting to these and so come to reject the less good (though this forming of standards may be a slow process, as parents looking at children's preferred books or listening to their preferred music often realise). Alternative activities can be proposed and encouraged: sports, swimming, music, ballet, chess, school and other societies. These may not necessarily have specific moral effects, though they are likely to give useful experience in relationships with other people, but they can certainly serve to avoid addictions to viewing or to other undesirable ways of spending time.

Beyond this there is further recourse to what Milton described, in his seventeenth-century denunciation of censorship,[19] as the principles of sound judgement which are the best protection of any state. What schools, and parents, can do is to develop these principles by encouraging critical thinking about what is being put forward by the mass media. The techniques of discussion earlier mentioned can use the material amply provided by popular programmes or magazines. Soap operas will already have stimulated pupils' opinions about their characters and their actions. Discussion of various episodes can certainly elicit moral values and help the group to realise which moral standards are relevant and which they prefer. (Again, the discussion technique has to be skilfully employed; one inspector of schools commented sadly that if some teachers applied to the discussion of a popular comic the methods they used in discussing Shakespeare, they could probably kill interest in the comic stone dead.) In fact many schools already are using materials provided by the mass media as the basis of discussion. Sometimes, this teaching is to safeguard against the wiles of advertisers, since analysis of advertisements can produce awareness of deception, insinuation, misleading claims. Sometimes it is rather a part of civic education, showing differences in the presentation of political or social information by various sources: analysis of the choice of words and types of statement found in these presentations reveals concealed bias. While it may be argued that young people need to have reached a certain degree of maturity before they can use the principles which are the best defence against moral, commercial or political corruption, and so they may have to be protected by some indirect censorship or at least by some control of the stimuli affecting them, it usually appears that they can develop sound judgement in moral and political matters likely to affect them even by the upper primary school stage.

EMOTIONAL COMPONENTS OF MORAL EDUCATION

The development of such techniques of discussion seems to have some promise for moral education, yet there remains doubt as to whether these school experiences will develop sound moral standards which will be acted on now and later. Here we find renewed emphasis on the need for emotional involvement to ensure appropriate behaviour. There recurs the assertion that moral behaviour is 'caught not taught'.

   The hidden curriculum of schools is certainly likely to be effective here. The values implicit in the teaching materials used by the school, in the school's rules and system of rewards and punishments are assimilated through experience even if not consciously registered. (On the conscious level, we might note that the value of 'fairness' does seem to be more explicitly stated and more often put into practice in schools than in the rest of society – is this a moral standard at variance with those of society? Schools' denunciations of cheating might also be thought at variance with some practices outside school – and in some school systems parents' advice to their children may run contrary to school advice on this point. In these respects schools perhaps set higher standards of morality than much of the rest of society.) Another part of the hidden curriculum, though sometimes it also is made highly explicit, is the value emphasised by the school peer-group of not telling tales. This value may well be approved in some social groups outside the school but it is one about which teachers may have divergent views.

The effect of the teacher's personality in transmitting moral values to pupils remains a debated area. In many societies, entrance to training as a teacher has required certificates from church authorities that the applicant is of good character: contracts of employment, in the past, have also sometimes speci-fied that the teacher's behaviour will conform to certain standards – no drinking or smoking in public, regular church attendance, for example. Clearly many societies have believed that the moral character of the teacher is likely to be imitated by the pupils. Yet now there is considerable support for the view that the private life of the teacher should not be subject to control or criticism by the teacher's employers or by parents, provided that the teacher's behaviour during school time is acceptable and professional.

But within school activities teachers do convey their own moral attitudes. Their truthfulness is evident, or absent, in dealings with pupils and colleagues. Their willingness to work conscientiously is one of the most easily assessed of their characteristics, from the point of view of pupils and other members of staff. Their respect for others, or lack of respect for them, is equally apparent. Their attitude to the subject or subjects they teach similarly reveals their standards of care, accuracy, reasonable-ness. It does not follow that teachers' good traits, rather than the less good, will be imitated: laziness on the part of the teacher is often contagious. There are also, of course, other personality traits – cheerfulness, a sense of humour – which are appreciated in a school and which may counterbalance other less desirable characteristics. Yet, for good or for ill, the moral principles of the teachers do play some part in the school's influence on pupils.

HOME CIRCUMSTANCES AND THE DEVELOPMENT OF MORALITY

Whatever the contribution made by the school curriculum, overt or hidden, to pupils' moral development, some writers would assert that the foundations of morality are established before this, by the emotional conditioning given by the home. In the mid-1950s, Margaret Knight[20] put forward the view, in radio broad-casts which, from today's perspective, aroused astonishingly impassioned hostility as well as approval, that the teaching of religion is not essential to moral education. Religion may in any case be rejected at adolescence and then morals may be rejected too. She argued that humanist education in a loving and supportive family is a fully satisfactory way of establishing morality. In the good family atmosphere, control of individual impulses, discipline, disinterestedness can be effectively developed. As to the question of the need for morality, she thought it could be adequately answered by pointing out that human beings are 'naturally social beings', who live in communities, and that the life in any community is much better when members are friendly and cooperative than when they are hostile and unhelpful. It also seemed to her that 'most people are prepared to accept as a completely self-evident moral axiom that we must not be completely selfish.' This argument certainly makes large assumptions about human nature and a general readiness to accept this 'moral axiom'. Yet the influence of the early years in the family is generally agreed to be very great and to affect subsequent morality. Schools might therefore be tempted to say that the matter of moral education is beyond their control and already provided for. But of course there remains the problem that not all children will experience the loving and supportive family atmosphere which is claimed to be so effective in establishing morality. There remains also the question of how complete and lasting such family conditioning is.

From the psychoanalytic point of view, early experience in the family has also been recognised as determining later morality in a rather different way. Bettelheim has emphasised[21] the importance for the child of the parents' example in accepting morality and the reality principle. He has further suggested that the anxiety caused by fear of loss of the parents' love is a powerful motivation for the child to learn, and to live up to the parents' moral standards. But children may meet with other standards in society and the standards of the peer-group especially may be less demanding than those of the parents. 'The mistake we still make is to hope that more and more citizens will have developed a mature morality, one they have critically tested against experience, without first having been subject as children to a stringent morality based on fear and trembling.' (Religious teaching, Bettelheim noted, formerly had similarly beneficial effects through inducing fear.)

From a different psychological orientation, but with something of the same reference back to early experience, conscience has also been described[22] as 'conditioned anxiety'.

THE DEVELOPMENT OF EMPATHY

The effectiveness of the family situation may be said to arise from the feelings that different members of the family have for each other and their ability to understand each other's feelings.

(Literature, and real life experience, of course give ample evidence that such sympathy and understanding do not always develop in families. One of the benefits indeed claimed for the kibbutz system has been that it freed people from the complex emotional problems of much family life.) Nevertheless, this early experience clearly does frequently lead to perception of others' responses and a capacity to 'feel with' them, even if the individual does not particularly sympathise with, or like, the other family members.

Whatever the family background of pupils and its effects in developing such perceptions and feelings, many schools are now concerned to foster the quality of empathy as a means of achieving good moral development. What is intended here is the ability to enter into the feelings of other people – not simply to know, or assume, what they are feeling but to have an emotional perception of their reactions.

The term 'empathy' is admittedly relatively new and its use still varies in different contexts. Originally it related to physical sensations, as when people feel – to a limited, and sometimes slight, extent – the muscular efforts which are being made by athletes whom they are watching. This 'feeling with' others has been extended to feeling something of the emotions of others, for example, feeling pleasure with the winners of a trophy: or the disappointment of someone who has just failed to win a prize. Empathy is thus to be distinguished from a term which is sometimes close to it in meaning, 'sympathy', for in sympathising we feel pity or compassion: empathising can take place with regard to any emotion.

In school subjects, most obviously literature attempts to evoke empathy with a wide range of characters: but it is also cultivated in some teaching of history, to make the events of the past more real and better understood. In social studies, cultivating empathy may be expected to arouse concern for other people or to reduce hostility towards them or, simply, to create awareness of shared traits and experiences. Methods of developing this characteristic are still rather uncertain. Normally, illustrations of others' experiences are provided, by pictures, documents, artefacts, films, and the individual is invited to try to enter into the experience of those others imaginatively. In some history lessons, for example, the experience of the past is re-created as nearly as possible by using an ancient building and typical furnishings of a chosen time, by dressing pupils in the costumes of that time and, possibly, by letting them prepare and eat a typical meal in these circumstances. This, it is believed, must produce a closer approximation to the experience of people in the past than does the cognitive study of historical events, or even of historical places, since now the learners may *feel* how people in the past felt. The most difficult aspect of such teaching is, however, to avoid simple projection of the individual's own experience which will prevent true realisation of others' experience: in the example cited, there would be the need to get away from the assumption that hot water is somewhere on tap and that this meal is 'different'. Thus, in such empathising, it is necessary to include cognitive data in the experience, to bear in mind, for example, the social hierarchy in which children would have found themselves, and to which they would have been accustomed, in past times. Similarly, in attempts to cultivate empathy with people of other nationalities, or people who differ greatly in age from the empathiser, there is need for cognitive skill in recognising the probable effects of national customs or of ageing: it is not enough simply to ask 'how would *I* feel in these circumstances?'

The assumption is thus made that by these techniques, and by the use of role-play, people can enter into the situation of others and will then behave better towards others because they have this understanding of them. Thus more moral action towards others is expected. Yet further study is needed to discover whether empathy can be fostered by teaching, whether it depends partly on individual differences: and whether indeed empathy does lead to more considerate and helpful behaviour towards others. It is certainly an important kind of learning where the integration of cognitive and emotional factors is vital.

TEACHERS AND MORAL EDUCATION

While individual teachers differ in the kind of moral education they offer by example, and while those teachers who are expected to teach morals directly do need careful training for the task, it still remains a general responsibility of schools to contribute to the moral education of their pupils. Otherwise pupils are left to contend as best they may with the pressures of the media and the peer-group, sometimes fortified by a good family background which will inculcate morality but sometimes with a family background which will be apathetic or immoral in various respects.

The reluctance of some schools and some teachers to intervene is comprehensible, especially as there is, as we have noted, a possible variety of opinions among teachers on some questions of morality. Nevertheless, we recall the Danish Council's principle that there are some points on which agreement is almost universal. But it has been asserted that too often schools fail to assert moral standards when they should do so. Sometimes they may believe that they will not have the support of their local authorities if they insist on applying sanctions to pupils who have acted immorally – and it does seem true that in some cases, this support has not been forthcoming. Yet schools could make a wider appeal for support in such cases, to central government or to teachers' organisations – or, in some instances, to parents' organisations – if the matter seemed worth the time and energy which it would probably take.

What also seems unhappily a reason for lack of action within some schools is lack of certainty that moral standards are worth supporting. Here occasionally one finds in some teachers an unthinking acceptance of the opinion that all moral standards are relative to a given time, society, or group within society (an opinion which is arguable) and that therefore, though it does not follow, all sets of 'moral' standards are equally good. Hence the excuse for inaction on the part of some teachers is that children should be left to adopt the standards of their social milieu and that it would be wrong to try to teach them 'middle-class morality'. In this way, an ill-defined swear-word serves to obscure the need to consider precisely what moral standards the pupils are learning, or should learn: it also serves to conceal the extent to which some moral principles are accepted by all social groups, are accepted in many countries, and have been accepted at different times in history. Certainly, schools can justify their teaching of certain moral standards only if they have carefully thought about these standards and are convinced of their value: they should not simply pass on their own prejudices. This thinking about standards is the kind of preparation all schools should make.

One writer[23] has accused some schools today of lack of nerve since they do not make clear their views about discipline and they fail to insist that moral principles be respected. Lack of nerve can obviously come from various causes – possibly from perception of the immense difficulties of educating emotion and reason to combine towards moral action. It should not be allowed to persist simply through muddled thinking, or sloth. Moral education is too important for that. It can of course be argued that moral education is not what teachers are specifically employed to give: their training is often largely irrelevant to this task. Yet society does expect moral influence to be exerted by the schools and schools have the rare characteristic of being in touch with practically the whole of the younger generation.

CONCLUSIONS

At present education of emotions and morals lacks the guidance of a clear theory of emotional development, though a number of psychological writings have tried to illuminate this area. There is also, in some countries, an absence of agreement about various aspects of moral behaviour. In this respect collective systems have an advantage in defining what is expected in interactions with others and in stating explicitly the norms of behaviour in the collective. Systems based on one religious creed have a similar advantage.

The influence of the family in both emotional and moral development is obviously of major importance. Schools therefore, in systems which are not collective or determined by one religious creed, have to recognise this influence and decide how far their educational policy agrees or should agree with that of the home. Child-centred educators, while convinced of the natural goodness of the child, still recognise that moral development may be complicated or distorted by adverse or contrary influences in the environment. Their theory may however make them more optimistic about the eventual outcome than those who believe that the child has no innately good qualities but is simply conditioned or shaped by the environment, and may have been too strongly affected by earlier experiences for change to be possible.

Some teachers are more directly involved with moral education than others, according to the subjects they teach and according to their designated post in a school – though any teacher may be consulted on moral issues by a pupil who finds that teacher understanding and feels the teacher's view would be worth having. For some teachers, the contribution made to moral education may be simply through the way in which their teaching is done and their own personality. All teachers, however, are likely to affect the emotional development of their pupils to some extent. By their contributions to general staff discussions of policy they may help to decide what stand the school takes on moral issues and what kind of environment the school offers.

The idea that morality is 'caught not taught' is both encouraging and discouraging for schools. If the statement is true, then, despite the uncertainties of method and curriculum, the atmosphere of the school and the attitudes of the teachers may produce the hoped-for results – assuming that the school atmosphere is good and the teachers morally acceptable. At the same time, it may also mean that other influences in society outside the school have been more influential and will continue to be more influential: in this case, unless the influences of the school and the home and neighbourhood are fortunately of the same kind, tending to the same effects, then the school may be able to offer only a short and evanescent experience of good emotional and moral surroundings. Such an offering still seems worth providing.

Questions

1. To what extent does traditional education seem to have contributed to the emotional development of the individual?

2. What arguments would suggest that the schools should offer education which is only cognitive?

3. What justifications can teachers in Western democracies offer for the moral principles they try to teach?

4. How satisfactory does Kohlberg's theory of the development of moral judgement seem to be?

5. What advantages seem to be present when the teaching of morals is linked to the teaching of religion?

6. How may parents limit the influence of the mass media on their children?

7. In what circumstances would the teaching of empathy seem likely to be particularly helpful?

8. To what extent, if any, should employers be concerned with the morality of individual teachers?

9. Is morality 'caught not taught'?

CHAPTER 8

Conclusions

The questions and problems we have surveyed confirm that education is a complicated affair. They confirm also the need for those engaged in education to be clear about what they intend to do and whether the results of their efforts are satisfactory. This need is not always self-evident. Many teachers – and many parents – can reasonably point out that for much of the time they are not making important policy decisions and they are engaged in fairly routine, specific activities. Yet even these routine activities result from an underlying decision to influence learners: the behaviour of parents or teachers in everyday circumstances depends on the view they have of the nature of the learners and their own role and responsibilities. Certainly this view is not constantly reconsidered or analysed: but it is present and influential.

We have noticed various educational situations in which there are differences of opinion among the people concerned. To deal effectively with such situations, it is necessary to state explicitly what the purposes of education are and to recognise which assumptions are being made about the nature of those being educated. Here the views of the individual teacher or educator may not seem to carry much weight but it still is important for them to be able to state their views and their reasons for holding these views. Individuals can be members of teacher organisations or parent associations which, collectively, are influential. Through these, individuals can propose or support changes in education which they consider necessary and right. Most governments nowadays claim to consult with such organisations and to give serious attention to their views. But the organisations' effectiveness depends on the general competence of their members to give reasonable and knowledgeable opinions. The effectiveness of a school similarly depends on the views of individual teachers.

Teachers' organisations in particular must be competent not only to respond to governmental enquiries about educational decisions but to initiate proposals for improvements in education. Even if changes have taken place in the conditions of entry to teaching and even if public opinion, and conditions of service, no longer demand that teachers be paragons of virtue, teachers remain a group within society which is above average in intelligence and which is hard-working and persevering – teachers have to have these qualities to some extent at least in order to achieve their basic qualifications and satisfy the authorities that they are acceptable entrants to the teaching profession. (Some individuals do diverge from this average by being lazy, uninterested, incompetent: but they are a small minority.) Moreover, teachers have the advantage of practical experience: their knowledge of the abilities and behaviour of children and young people is realistic: this enables them to assess theories of education and proposals for change in education and to foresee the probable responses of pupils (and of parents) to new developments. Hence teacher organisations can claim, as professional groups, to be the best qualified to advise on, and recommend, educational policy decisions – provided always that the teachers' professional preparation, and subsequent studies, have given due attention to the theory of education.

MAJOR DECISIONS

Interpretations of human nature

A basic decision has to be made as to the view of human nature which is accepted. Much depends on whether the educator trusts to the presence of good qualities in all children – e.g., curiosity, interest in learning, ability to be creative – and expects the human being who is given the right learning environment to develop also good relationships with other people: or whether the educator considers that human beings have to be firmly guided towards the right kind of learning, have to be prevented from developing anti-social behaviours and must be carefully taught to accept the rules which society has constructed for its members. It is important whether the educator thinks the development of the individual is the major aim or whether the educator accepts that the human being can exist happily only as an accepted member of society, working for the good of other members of society.

These basic decisions also depend on whether the educator accepts a religious interpretation of human life which defines the characteristics of human beings and proposes the desired outcome of education. Similarly, some political creeds provide an interpretation of human nature and an indication of the purposes of education.

Interpretations of the teacher's role

From these decisions come differing interpretations of the teacher's role, as we have seen on various occasions. The child-centred teacher will be much more careful to respect the learner's interests and to give the learner responsibilities in decision-making. The teacher educating in a collective system will be more concerned with the learner's development as a good member of the group and will speak with the authority of the group. Other teachers may see themselves as scientifically applying behaviourist techniques to shape the responses of the learners. Others again may consider themselves interpreters of religious doctrines, leading the young to acceptance and observance of the true faith. The authority which society gives to teachers and the definitions of role which it provides, e.g., in statements of terms of appointment to teaching posts, will also depend on the prevailing educational theory of the society – in some cases, as we have observed, there may be some incompatibility in the teachers' interpretation of their role and society's interpretation: in others, the two will coincide.

Deciding on rights

Decisions as to the rights of children, parents and society also rest on the chosen interpretation of human nature. Where belief is placed on the innate potential of the child, the rights of children are likely to be given high priority, superseding those of society in some instances and superseding those of parents. Where it is believed that education must make children into good members of society, greater emphasis will be given to the rights of society to make decisions and such decisions may involve over-riding parents' preferences and wishes. Where, as often happens, there is no clear expression of educational theory, then the rights accorded respectively to the child, the parents and the agents of society remain controversial. The teacher's readiness to respect parental rights in education must depend on the values the teacher sets on the 'free' development of the individual child or on the duty of making children good members of society or followers of a chosen religious faith.

Looking for empirical evidence

These choices of interpretations are value judgements. It is not possible to discover objectively which characteristics are 'natural' to human beings since, as we have noted, so much depends on the environment in which they develop and since influences from other people affect them from the very beginning of life.

Yet some evidence is present in the results of applying different theories of education, in one or other country or school, in the past or present. Here we do find apparent differences in outcome: but it still remains difficult to discover whether the

Israeli kibbutz, for instance, achieves all its educational aims and produces the intended kind of person or whether failures in the application of the collective theory make it less effective than was intended. In all educational systems, there are the variables of the country's economic, geographical and social circumstances. The defeat of Nazi Germany and the experiences immediately following that defeat make it difficult to decide precisely how effective was the collective system of education which the Nazi government was developing – and whether, ultimately, it would have achieved its ends. Some apparently surviving 'successes' may have been caused by pre-Nazi historical factors. Similarly, economic affluence at a certain point in a country's history may produce apparent success of education for individual development, while times of economic crisis may lead to belief that such a policy is a failure and education concentrating on the needs of the state is essential.

Where empirical studies of the achievements of pupils in different countries have been made, no one country is consistently the best in producing high levels of achievement, though some, for example, Japan, do tend frequently to appear higher in performance levels than others. But these studies focus mainly on recognised school subjects: they therefore do not give information about the more general, long-term effects of the educational systems. Such information may be gained from descriptive reports by writers on comparative education, which suggest that in fact educational systems do have a marked effect in instilling some values related to study and culture. They suggest that some personality characteristics are thus strengthened or disregarded, e.g. thoroughness, intellectual arrogance, emphasis on many-sided learning. But in every educational system we find also that there are internal criticisms of the system. Parents want better conditions for their children, politicians urge greater efforts to produce good citizens, standards of work and attitudes to working are said to be unsatisfactory. It seems impossible to find a country which is wholly satisfied with its education system (perversely, we may find this reassuring). Practically all are engaged in processes of reform. Teacher education in particular is an area in which criticisms and changes are most frequent. Hence, while comparative and historical studies suggest that the aims set for education and the attitudes adopted towards children do have perceptible and important results, the evidence is not such as to prove or disprove the interpretation of human nature underlying different systems or to show the goodness or badness of the intended and at least partially achieved outcomes. The evidence possibly suggests that indeed much education is 'caught not taught' and that young people in many countries develop similar attitudes because they pick them up from those around them – and people everywhere behave in a characteristically 'human' way. Formal reports on education on a large or small scale do not give full information as to what is in fact happening: many educational ventures probably fail to achieve their purpose because they fail to consider and analyse what really are the major influences on the development of the young. (It is perhaps significant that when individuals claim to have had a 'good' education, they normally refer to the effects of an individual school or, especially, to the influence of one or two good teachers, rather than to any formal system or theory.)

Is indoctrination legitimate?

Since there is this absence of 'proof' of the rightness of any chosen theory of education, some people question whether we have the right to make decisions as to the principles and behaviours we try to produce in children and young people. This query seems to result from misinterpretations of the meaning of 'indoctrination'. If we take no action to educate, we are still indoctrinating in a negative way, by suggesting that what young people or learners do is a matter of indifference. If we decide to teach, then we do 'indoctrinate'. But, as we noted earlier, what seems to be objected to is the kind of situation where children or other individuals are taught without realising that they are being taught or what they are being taught. In such cases, they do not have the opportunity to think critically about what is being put into their minds or their behaviour. This is the 'bad' form of indoctrination (though as we have noted also, there may be some such indoctrination which is necessary before children have reached the stage at which they can think things out – looking both ways before crossing the road is something where indoctrination at an early age has much to be said for it).

It is true, as we have also noted, that the attitudes of the teacher do convey themselves to the learners, even if this is not consciously intended. (In this respect it is interesting to consider what teachers convey to children by their style of dress, their appearance, by the badges or other symbols of beliefs they wear. Some teachers argue that they have a right, as individuals, to proclaim their adherence to a religious or political group, or to wear a CND badge, for example. Yet is this an instance of the kind of indoctrination which does not give the pupil a chance for rational examination of the principle being propagated?) So, too, the attitudes of parents convey themselves to children either through casual remarks or expressions or through behaviour. Some indoctrination of these kinds is inevitable. All the educator can do, for the protection of the learner, is to observe learners' reactions so as to discover what has been unintentionally taught.

At the same time, we must recognise that this concern about indoctrination presupposes certain beliefs about the nature of human beings and of education. In some countries and according to some religious teaching, education is not a matter of submitting ideas to the rational judgement of the learner. There are some principles which must be accepted and which are not subject to human reasoning or individual reinterpretation. Hence the earnest desire of many educators has been to indoctrinate by whatever methods may cause learning to be prompt, lasting and efficacious. Present criticisms of this emotional or prescriptive teaching arise from acceptance of the view that the individual should be given freedom of choice and encouraged to use her or his critical judgement on all that is taught. They represent certain value judgements.

Avoiding personal bias

Since educators make value judgements it is worrying that they may be judging in too narrow a way and allowing themselves to be influenced too greatly by their own prejudices. More than one thinker (notably Francis Bacon[1]) has pointed out the inherent weaknesses of human thinking and its tendency to be misled by words, by theories, by personal experiences. All that can be done here is to consider the conclusions arrived at by other people – making allowances for *their* personal bias and tendency to be misled by words and theories. In this way it is at least possible to discover where differences occur and then to deduce where personal experiences may be causing bias. If, for example, an educator is convinced of the goodness of human nature and the good results of letting children have freedom, does this view seem due to working with an unrepresentative sample of young people, at some age levels only, or, possibly, to overlooking the amount of influence the educator's own personality is having? Is the educator who admires the rigorous training in citizenship in some states the kind of person who would have been particularly happy in such a system and therefore assumes it would suit everyone? Most simply, in thinking about education, how many people judge from the schools they themselves attended or have worked in – just as they judge the qualities of family life from their own experience in a good (or not so good) family? These kinds of bias are fairly easy to identify: and can be reduced to a considerable extent by looking for wider and more representative information about experiences. Comparison with reports of others' experience can show where personal bias is likely. At the same time, discovery of views similar to one's own in people who have had very different background experiences may possibly give confidence that personal bias is not being influential and the views have general validity.

Being eclectic

There are great attractions in being a whole-hearted adherent of one chosen educational theory. Yet although, in the past, the theory of one or other of the great writers on education has been presented to teachers as the ideal, there seems at present, for most teachers, little chance of finding anyone who provides equally satisfactorily for all aspects of education. Hence we reach, perhaps reluctantly, the conclusion that today's teacher has to derive some inspiration from one educator, some interpretations of human development from another, and the formulation of aims from more than one source. This eclecticism is not necessarily undesirable, provided that the teacher, or parent, is consistent about underlying principles.

Eclecticism is necessary also when educators look to various social sciences for information and enrichment. In the nineteenth century it was believed that philosophy could provide the aims for education while psychology could provide the knowledge of human nature necessary for finding methods of achieving these aims. Philosophy today is no longer looked to for aims – educators can provide their own – though philosophical analysis of concepts and arguments can sometimes contribute to the educator's own analyses of ideas and educational slogans. Psychology has not yet succeeded in producing an agreed body of knowledge explaining all the characteristics of human beings: it has rather divided into various schools (as we have noticed in passing), each possibly contributing something of interest to our understanding (and possibly, as in the case of behaviourism, something to help with teaching methods). Sociology, on the large scale dealing with society outside schools, and on the smaller scale, with societies in schools and in the classroom, has certainly provided useful insights for educators, showing the relevance of structures outside and inside schools, and the home and neighbourhood circumstances of those being educated. The history of education makes it possible to see changes in education, and especially in the curriculum: it shows also changes in acceptance of responsibility for the provision of schools and other educational institutions. The history of educational ideas is one of the most stimulating ways of discovering which ideas seem of constant value and which ideas are rather representative of our own particular time and society, possibly merely passing fashions. Comparative education is also admirably useful in showing other theories at work and, possibly, discovering which methods seem successful. With regard to methods, too, educational research in our own and other countries is naturally an important source of guidance. Hence the reasonableness for the educator of being eclectic in looking at the contributions of each of these branches of study.

REACHING AGREEMENT ON THEORY OF EDUCATION

Given the need to be eclectic in many ways, individual teachers and parents may worry that agreement is unlikely to be reached when they meet with their colleagues and peers. Other educators may, it can be feared, have very different ideas. It is true that differences in underlying beliefs about human nature must cause people to differ considerably in some of their proposals for education. In these difficult circumstances, the present advocacy of rational discussion has much to commend it. If people can make it clear to the others concerned what their intentions in education are, and what effects they hope to produce, it is likely that useful agreement can be achieved in many cases. If there is an irreducible conflict of principle, then it is at least helpful to know what it is: subsequent action must depend on the authority given to one or other party to safeguard the rights of the child and/or the rights of society. In fact, in the teaching profession, given a common background of studies in education, and a common background of experience in working with children and young people, disagreements are likely to be less frequent than might at first seem probable. What is needed in schools is more opportunity to discuss such questions, in circumstances where discussion is not inhibited by wanting to get home at a reasonable time or by the knowledge that a serious comment will not be well received. If such discussions are to succeed, they can well centre on the individual school's own objectives and the extent to which they are being achieved. This kind of discussion should give the school necessary confidence in taking a stand on matters of discipline, in exchanges with the governing body and with local and other authorities. If the staff of a school have the chance to discuss suitably, in groups or as a whole, the success of the school in carrying out its purposes, and changes which could lead to greater success, this can be the best form of teacher appraisal. It is much more likely than any other to lead to changes for the better, while avoiding individual discouragement: self-appraisal by this means is most likely to be accurate and effective.

In such considerations, we are of course assuming that there is no official directive as to the educational theory which must be accepted by all teachers. In Western democracies, teachers do have an advantage in being left considerable freedom to decide their own educational views and even to act on them: though in any society, it is what the teacher believes about the purpose of education that will be influential, whether there is an official theory or not. Decisions about the best theory of education thus remain, ultimately, with the individual teacher.

Consultation with colleagues serves to give new ideas and to check one's existing ideas: so do reading and wider educational conferences: but there are probably some points on which the individual will want to differ, both from actual colleagues, and from those who have written and spoken about education. What is important is to recall, from time to time, what the underlying principles are and to relate them to the latest public controversy in education, to various problem pupils, to proposals for further reforms of the educational system. Such considerations and discussions occur intermittently. Teachers, and parents, still spend most of their time working with individuals, observing them from hour to hour, making immediate practical arrangements for their progress: it is easy to become absorbed in the daily routine. Yet recalling and revising at suitable times and intervals one's own individual theory of education gives coherence, value and enjoyment to this demanding and never-ending process.

Questions

1. Which situations in school life are likely to require consideration of educational theories?

2. Which view of the nature of children seems to you the most acceptable?

3. What is your interpretation of the teacher's role?

4. In what cases do you see possible conflicts between the rights of children, parents' rights and the rights of society? On what principles would you resolve such conflicts?

5. What further information from the social sciences would be useful in revising or refining your definitions of the purposes of education?

REFERENCES

(All places of publication are London unless otherwise stated)

Chapter 2

1. Rousseau J-J 1762 *Emile*. Flammarion, Paris, 1930
2. Spencer H 1929 *Education, Intellectual, Moral and Physical*. Watts & Co.
3. Bazeley E 1948 *Homer Lane and the Little Commonwealth*. New Education Book Club
4. Neill A S 1937 *That Dreadful School*. H. Jenkins; see also Croall J 1983 *Neill of Summerhill*. Routledge & Kegan Paul
5. Froebel F 1887 *The Education of Man*. Appleton
6. Lane H 1948 *Talks to Parents and Teachers*. George Allen and Unwin
7. Wills D 1945 *The Barns Experiment*. George Allen and Unwin; see also Wills W D 1964 *Homer Lane*. Allen and Unwin
8. Pestalozzi J H 1901 *Leonard and Gertrude*, translated by Channing E. Heath
9. Alain (Chartier E) 1959 *Propos sur l'Education*. Presses Universitaires de France, Paris (First published 1932)
10. Goldman R J 1965 *Readiness for Religion*. Routledge & Kegan Paul
11. A report of the Central Advisory Council for Education (England) 1967 *Children and Their Primary Schools*. HMSO. (The Plowden Report)
12. Illich I 1973 *Deschooling Society*. Penguin Education Specials
13. Ariès P 1973 *Centuries of Childhood*. Penguin Books (First published 1960)
14. Montessori M 1917 *The Advanced Montessori Method*. Heinemann
15. Department of Education and Science and the Welsh Office 1981 *The School Curriculum*. HMSO
16. Bennett N 1976 *Teaching Styles and Pupil Progress*. Open Press
17. Eggleston J F, Galton M, Jones M 1976 *Process and Products of Science Teaching*. Macmillan/Schools Council
18. Galton M, Simon B, Croll P 1980 *Inside the Primary Classroom*. Routledge & Kegan Paul

Chapter 3

1. Knox J First Book of Discipline, *Works* 1846–64, ed. D Laing, Edinburgh, reprint AMS Press
2. Plato *The Republic*, translated Lindsay A D, 1942. J. M. Dent

3. Spencer H 1850 'National education', *Social Statics*. Robert Schalkenbach Foundation 1954 New York
4. Board of Education 1937 *Handbook of Suggestions for Teachers*. HMSO, pp 9–11
5. See especially Dewey J 1916 *Democracy and Education*. Macmillan
6. Hendry J 1986 *Becoming Japanese*. Manchester University Press
7. Makarenko A S *The Road to Life*. Foreign Languages Publishing House, Moscow, 1951. And Makarenko A S *Problems of Soviet School Education*. Progress Publishers, Moscow, 1965
8. Günther K-H *et al* 1979 *Das Bildungswesen der Deutschen Demokratischen Republik*. Volkseigener Verlag, Berlin, pp 73–4
9. Hargreaves D 1982 *The Challenge for the Comprehensive School*. Routledge & Kegan Paul
10. Central Council of Education 1978 *U 90: Danish Educational Planning and Policy in a Social Context at the End of the Twentieth Century*. Schultz Forlag, Copenhagen, pp 100–9
11. Department of Education and Science and the Welsh Office 1984, Circular 3/84 and 21/84 HMSO, p 9

Chapter 4

1. Central Statistical Office 1987 *Social Trends* HMSO, vol 17
2. Befu H 1986 'The social and cultural background of child development in Japan and the United States', in Stevenson H, Azuma H, Hakuta K (eds) 1986 *Child Development and Education in Japan*. W. H. Freeman, New York, p 20
3. *International Yearbook of Education* 1986 *Primary Education on the Threshold of the Twenty-first Century*. UNESCO, vol XXXVIII p 16
4. Alain (Emile Chartier) 1959 *Propos sur l'Education*. Presses Universitaires de France, Paris
5. Quintilian *Institutio Oratoria* translated by Butler H E. Loeb; see also Rusk R R, Scotland J 1969 *Doctrines of the Great Educators*. Macmillan, Ch. 3
6. *Times Educational Supplement* 7 Nov. 1986, p 19
7. Beattie N 1985 *Professional Parents*. Falmer Press
8. *Times Educational Supplement* 13 Dec. 1985
9. Taylor Report 1977 *A New Partnership for Our Schools*. HMSO
10. Locke J 1690 *Some Thoughts Concerning Education*. Ward Lock
11. Spock B 1946 *Baby and Child Care*. Pocket Books, New York
12. *The Daily Telegraph* 17 Oct. 1986, p 36

Chapter 5

1. Watson J B 1919 *Psychology From the Standpoint of a Behaviorist*. Norton, New York. Reprint 1983 Longwood Publishing Group
2. For fuller discussion of stimulus-reflex theories see Hall C S, Lindzey G 1957 *Theories of Personality*. Wiley, Ch. 11
3. Thorndike E L 1932 *The Fundamentals of Learning*. Teachers College, New York
4. Valentine C W 1957 *The Normal Child*. Pelican Books
5. Skinner B F 1971 *Beyond Freedom and Dignity*. Cape, p 199; Skinner

B F 1978 *Reflections on Behaviorism and Society*. Prentice-Hall
6. Rosenow E 1980 'Rousseau's *Emile*, an anti-Utopia', *British Journal of Educational Studies* XXVIII, 3: 212–24

Chapter 6

1. Consultative Committee on the Curriculum (Scottish Education Department) 1977 *Structure of the Curriculum in the Third and Fourth Year of the Scottish Secondary School* (the Munn Report). HMSO
2. Small R 1984 The Concept of Polytechnical Education. *British Journal of Educational Studies* XXXII, 1: 27–44
3. *Le Monde de l'Education* mai 1981, p 23
4. Günther K-H *et al.* 1979 *Das Bildungswesen der Deutschen Demokratischen Republik*. Volkseigener Verlag, Berlin, p 83
5. Report of the Committee of Inquiry appointed by the Secretary of State for Education and Science under the Chairmanship of Sir Alan Bullock FBA 1975 *A Language for Life*. HMSO
6. Hirst P H 1974 *Moral Education in a Secular Society*. University of London Press
7. Torney J *et al.* 1975 *Civic Education in Ten Countries* International Studies in Evaluation VI. Almqvist & Wiksell
8. Department of Education and Science and Welsh Office 1984 *Initial Teacher Training: Approval of Courses*, Circular No 3/84 and 21/84. HMSO
9. Department of Education and Science 1983 *Teaching in Schools: The Content of Initial Training*. HMSO
10. See Torney, as in reference 7 above
11. UNESCO 1974 *A Recommendation Concerning Education for International Understanding, Co-operation and Peace and Education Relating to Human Rights and Fundamental Freedoms*. Department of Education and Science 1976 Circular 9/76
12. Peters R S 1972 in Dearden R F, Hirst P H, Peters R S (eds) *Education and the Development of Reason*. Routledge & Kegan Paul
13. Hirst P H 1974 *Knowledge and the Curriculum*. Routledge & Kegan Paul
14. Phenix P 1964 *Realms of Meaning*. McGraw-Hill, New York
15. Lawton D 1975 *Class, Culture and the Curriculum*. Routledge & Kegan Paul
16. For an account of Herbart's theory see Rusk R R, Scotland J 1969 *Doctrines of the Great Educators*. Macmillan, Ch. 9
17. Department of Education and Science 1978 *Primary Education in England: A Survey by HM Inspectors of Schools*. HMSO
18. Dearden R F 1984 *Theory and Practice in Education*. Routledge & Kegan Paul, p 163
19. Dearden R F 1976 *Problems of Primary Education*. Routledge & Kegan Paul

Chapter 7

1. Neill A S 1939 *The Problem Teacher*. H. Jenkins, p 159
2. Dewey J 1934 'My pedagogic creed', Article IV, in Archambault,

R D 1974 *John Dewey on Education* University of Chicago Press
3. Spencer H 1850 *Social Statics* Robert Schalkenbach Foundation, 1954, p 314
4. Locke J 1690 *Some Thoughts Concerning Education*. Ward Lock
5. Suttie I 1935 *Origins of Love and Hate*. Kegan Paul
6. James W 1890 *Principles of Psychology*. Holt, New York
7. Erikson E H 1965 *Childhood and Society*. Penguin Books
8. Krathwohl D R, Bloom B B, Masia B B 1964 *Taxonomy of Educational Objectives: Affective Domain*. Longman
9. Central Council of Education 1978 *U 90: Danish Educational Planning and Policy in a Social Context at the End of the Twentieth Century*. Schultz Forlag, Copenhagen, pp 100–9
10. Bretagne C 1971 L'affaire de Médréac: les héros s'expliquent, *Elle* 22 février
11. *The Daily Telegraph* 17 Sept. 1986 and *The Daily Telegraph* 18 Sept. 1986
12. *The Times Educational Supplement* 7 Nov. 1986, p 19
13. Piaget J 1965 *The Moral Judgement of the Child*. Free Press; see also Duska R. Whelan M 1975 *A Guide to Piaget and Kohlberg*. Paulist Press
14. Kohlberg L 1976 in Lickona T (ed.) *Moral Development and Behaviour*, Holt Rinehart & Winston; see also Kohlberg L 1983 *The Psychology of Moral Development*. Harper & Row
15. See for example Stenhouse L, Verma G K, Wild R D, Nixon J 1982 *Teaching about Race Relations*. Routledge & Kegan Paul
16. Hirst P H 1974 *Moral Education in a Secular Society*. University of London Press
17. Jenkins D *et al*. 1980 *Chocolate, Cream, Soldiers*. The New University of Ulster, Occasional Papers
18. For a fuller discussion of this evolution see Sutherland M B 1972 *Everyday Imagining and Education*. Routledge & Kegan Paul
19. Milton J 1644 *Areopagitica*. Reprinted 1972, Saifer
20. Knight M 1955 *Morals Without Religion*. Dennis Dobson, pp 49–50
21. Bettelheim B 1970 in Sizer N F, Sizer T R (eds) *Moral Education: Five Lectures*. Harvard University Press, p 87
22. Eysenck H J 1975 in Lickona T (ed.) *Moral Development and Behavior*, Holt Rinehart & Winston, pp 108–23
23. Wilson J 1981 *Discipline and Moral Education*. NFER/Nelson

Chapter 8

1. Bacon F 1620 *Novum Organon* XLII in Robertson J M (ed.) *The Philosophical Works of Francis Bacon*, 1905. George Routledge, p 264

RECOMMENDED READING

Chapter 2

Ariès P 1973 *Centuries of Childhood*. Penguin Books

Bazeley E 1948 *Homer Lane and the Little Commonwealth*. New Education Book Club

Bennett N 1976 *Teaching Styles and Pupil Progress*. Open Press

Croall J 1983 *Neill of Summerhill*. Routledge and Kegan Paul

Dale R 1979 'From endorsement to disintegration: Progressive education from the Golden Age to the Green Paper', *British Journal of Educational Studies* XXVII **3** 191–209

Illich I 1973 *Deschooling Society*. Penguin Books

Lane H 1948 *Talks to Parents and Teachers*. George Allen and Unwin

Neill A S 1937 *That Dreadful School*. H. Jenkins: and Neill A S 1945 *Hearts not Heads in the School*. H. Jenkins

Rousseau J-J 1762 *Emile*

Spencer H 1850 *Moral Education* in *Education, Intellectual, Moral and Physical*. Watts and Co. 1929

Wills W D 1945 *The Barns Experiment*. George Allen and Unwin

Wills W D 1964 *Homer Lane*. Allen and Unwin

Chapter 3

Alain 1932 *Propos sur l'Education*. Presses Universitaires de France, Paris

Bettelheim B 1969 *The Children of the Dream*. Thames and Hudson

Central Council of Education 1978 *U 90: Danish Educational Planning and Policy in a Social Context at the End of the Twentieth Century*. Schultz Forlag, Copenhagen, pp 100–109

Dewey J 1916 *Democracy and Education*. MacMillan

Grant N 1979 *Soviet Education*. Penguin Books

Hendry J 1986 *Becoming Japanese*. Manchester University Press

King E 1979 *Other Schools and Ours* (5th edn). Holt, Rinehart and Winston, Chs 9, 10, 11

Makarenko A S *Problems of Soviet School Education*. Progress Publishers, Moscow 1965

Tiger L, Shepher J 1977 *Women in the Kibbutz*. Peregrine Books

Chapter 4

Beattie N 1985 *Professional Parents*. Falmer Press

Locke J *Some Thoughts Concerning Education*. Ward Lock

Macbeth A *et al*. 1982 *Scottish School Councils: policy-making, partici-
pation or irrelevance*; and 1986 *Parental Choice of School in Scotland*.
Department of Education, University of Glasgow
Taylor B 1983 *A Parent's Guide to Education*. Consumers' Association
and Hodder and Stoughton
Taylor Report 1977 *A New Partnership for our Schools*. HMSO

Chapter 5

Fontana D (ed.) 1984 *Behaviourism and Learning Theory in Education*.
Scottish Academic Press
Hall C S, Lindzey G 1957 *Theories of Personality*. Wiley Ch. 11
Skinner B F 1971 *Beyond Freedom and Dignity*. Cape
Skinner B F 1978 *Reflections on Behaviorism and Society*. Prentice-Hall

Chapter 6

Cox E 1983 *Problems and Possibilities for Religious Education*. Hodder
and Stoughton
Dearden R F 1984 *Theory and Practice in Education*. Routledge and
Kegan Paul
Heater D B 1984 *Peace Through Education*. Falmer Press
Musgrove F 1982 *Education and Anthropology*. Wiley
Pring R 1984 *Personal and Social Education in the Curriculum*. Hodder
and Stoughton
Torney J *et al*. 1975 *Civic education in ten countries* International Studies
in Evaluation, VI. Almqvist & Wiksell
UNESCO 1974 *A Recommendation Concerning Education for Inter-
national Understanding, Co-operation and Peace and Education
Relating to Human Rights and Fundamental Freedoms*
Watts A G 1983 *Education, Unemployment and the Future of Work*.
Open University Press

Chapter 7

Duska R, Whelan M 1975 *A Guide to Piaget and Kohlberg*. Paulist Press
Hirst P H 1974 *Moral Education in a Secular Society*. University of
London Press
Jenkins D *et al*. 1980 *Chocolate, Cream, Soldiers*. Occasional papers,
The New University of Ulster
Knight M 1955 *Morals without Religion*. Dennis Dobson
Wilson J 1981 *Discipline and Moral Education*. NFER/Nelson

INDEX